S0-BPU-448

FISH TALES

To Patrick and Julie —
Best wishes to old friends,
and good fishing!

Ron Gowe

FISH TALES

An autobiography of a
life growing up fishing in
Minnesota, and an
instruction manual, with
some good stories along
the way.

Ron Gower

NORTH STAR PRESS OF ST. CLOUD, INC.

Saint Cloud, Minnesota

Copyright © 2011 Author's Name

ISBN: 0-87839-426-5
ISBN-13: 978-0-87839-426-5

All rights reserved.

This is a work of fiction. Names, characters, places, and incidents are the products of the author's imagination or are used fictitiously. Any resemblance to actual events or persons, living or dead, is entirely coincidental.

First Edition, June 2011

Printed in the United States of America

Published by
North Star Press of St. Cloud, Inc.
P.O. Box 451
St. Cloud, Minnesota 56302

www.northstarpress.com

 # ACKNOWLEDGEMENTS

PPR and I wish to thank John Cross, Terry Davis and John Solensten for reading and commenting (and correcting) the early drafts, and to Corinne and Seal at North Star Press for their efficiency, kindness and beautiful work, as well as Doug Ohman for the perfect photo. As always, most thanks to my wife Anne, first for reading and helping with the ms, and before that for tolerating my fishing addiction for 50 years.

PERSONAE:

Professor Piscator Redux (**PPR**): An ancestor of Izaak Walton, growing up in Minnesota, or a figment of the **Reader**'s imagination.

> **PPR**: Also the author, a professor and fisherman who sometimes tells the truth.

Reader: A prospective book-buyer and novice fisherman seeking advice; aka: You

THE CONFERENCE

Reader: And why, pray tell, should I waste this evening on yet another of the infinite river of fish books? I could better spend my time at a dusky hatch, or even at my bench devising cunning flies to greet the dawn trout.

Piscator Redux/Redundas: As that most Complete ancestor of mine says, we anglers all love each other, and therefore we should feel it only brotherly to tell each other's tales.

R: I think Izaak was talking about killing otters, not reading fish stories.

PPR: Well, he's talking to Venator, a hunter, so he's just being agreeable; also otters kill fish, so he's eager to help wipe them out.

R: Doesn't sound like a catch-and-release story, does it? Anyway, I've read Walton, and Hemingway, Gingrich and Wulff, and lots of others. Isn't that enough? Now I want to go fishing.

PPR: But the reason you will doubtless fish well is because of all you've learned from reading all the experts on angling, and surely there is pleasure in their telling as well, and yet more to glean from yet another treatise on the gentle art of the angle.

R: And just what qualifies you to improve or even add to that lineup?

PPR: Well, I am a professor...

R: Oh God! Of literature, I suppose. Another dreamy escapist without a clue to real fishing, except what you've read. Why is it half the books on fishing are by professors of literature, and why should I waste my time on dreamy drivel of Wordsworthian nature when what I want is a way to catch a 22-inch brown?

PPR: (Hurt) Well, one needn't be abusive. I only mentioned it because I've had time, as a professor, to fish more than most people do in modern times; it's as close to being a full-time piscator as one can get these days. Also, it means I know how to write.....

R: For PMLA maybe. About fishing, I'll believe it when I read it.

PPR: AS I WAS SAYING, I can at least write proper English. Just read a bit before you go fishing, or after. Like all fishermen, I just want to share my stories with that great camaraderie that is part of the noble sport. We should all share our experiences, for, as Walton says, all fishermen love one another, and....

R: Yeh, yeh, yeh. Well, I'll give it a shot, just so I can be on my way to fish or hunt otters or anything else later on. Now since you're a prof as well as a fisherman, I expect this book will be full of "stretchers" and not a real how-to of fishing, right?

PPR: Sire, this is a true and righteous account of my life as a fisherman and an honest man.

R: Contradiction? Oxymoron?

PPR: Judge for yourself, sire, and if it is not all that it's advertised you can trade it for a copy of A River Runs Through It....

R: By another English professor, although I admit he at least tells a good story. Can't I just get my money back?

PPR: Just buy the book, brother angler!

R: OK. It's too late to go fishing now, anyway. Thanks a lot.

PPR: You're welcome. Actually, it's not really black-dark yet, and if you try a small caddis instead of the PED you may have some luck.

R: I can't see to tie it on. Think I'll go read the damn book instead.

(And so the Mariner hath his way)

AN INTRODUCTION TO THE AUTHOR

Y ES, I CONFESS TO HAVING BEEN FOR thirty-some years a professor of literature. Whether that makes me one of Walton's "contemplative men" or not is uncertain; what is true is that it gave me leisure for fishing and legitimate reason for reading much of the literature of angling, some of which is arguably among the lists of "great books."

My life in fishing actually began almost at the beginning. I was born in St. Paul, Minnesota, a propitious state for a budding fisherman, with the highest percentage of fishermen per capita in the country. Further, when I was a mere babe, my parents moved into a cottage on Lake Owasso in the St. Paul city limits, and some of my earliest memories, and strangely most vivid, considering I was barely an infant, are of the lake: a box turtle's belly, glistening in the water; toddling on a sandy beach, with that tangy, slightly fetid smell of a small mud-bottom lake; and, although I do not remember it, walking straight out into that water, without hesitation, up over my small head, until my father pulled me out.

We moved shortly into the city, but from that portentous beginning came my love affair with water, and ultimately the creatures that lived in it. Whether something was implanted in that infant fishbrain, or whether I was trained into it, fishing was from early on not just an interest but almost a necessity, and through various permutations it's been a constant in all my seventy years. Herbert Hoover, in *Fishing For Fun*, includes fishing in the list of important things that recur in spite of war, famine, plague, and all the other disasters that interrupt mankind. Though not so dramatically, I think of fishing in my life the same way: through the hormonal teens, into years of college, military service, family and children and profession, and ultimately retirement fishing has been a constant. It's changed forms, and was obviously not continuous, but the idea, the set of syanpses, was constantly programmed to chase some kind of fish. There have even been times when, like Jim Harrison, I knew I'd go literally crazy if I didn't fish.

Looked at objectively, reasonably (as my dear wife occasionally tries to do), this in itself is insane. I've spent a sizable proportion of my life, and my income, trying to outwit an almost prehistoric creature with a brain like a BB—and very often lost. I can in no way justify fishing as a way of filling the larder: the cost of eating a single Montana trout has often been equivalent to remodelling a good part of the house—again something Anne has only occasionally reminded me. Since most of my fishing has turned to catch and release as well, the statistics are even worse. In what has been for the most part a fairly normal, orderly and respectable life, the quest for conquest over various water-dwellers must appear a streak of total insanity.

And again my wife has mentioned this, but only rarely, usually when I've gone way beyond the appointed time to be home for the sake of "just one more cast." She knows my habits well enough to suspect it's just a case of a late hatch, or long walk to the car; yet understandably worries, especially as I get older. I always regret that, and vow to get back in time, and am doing better—sometimes.

A word more about Anne. She is a a fisherperson as well, and we've spent lots of time together fishing, although she's never become a trouter, nor does she have anything of my compulsiveness about the sport. But she does know what it's like, and has been amazingly tolerant of my aberration; it's at least a fairly harmless form of insanity, and she lives with it as she does most of my frailties, with patience and good humor. No fisherman could ask more.

 # KID FISHING

My DAD WAS AN ENTHUSIASTIC and not very good fisherman. Born in England, and raised in this country by a rigid, itinerant Methodist preacher father, he had none of the Presbyterian fly-fishing instruction of a Norman MacLean, nor was fishing even allowed on Sundays. Still he grew up in rural Minnesota, and somewhere along the way discovered the pleasures of panfish, both the sport and the eating. When I came along, I became his partner in long afternoons of worm-fishing. There are lots of small lakes around St. Paul, of course, and we sometimes even ranged out to Atwater or Stillwater, and occasionally we fished the backwaters of the Mississippi that rolled through town. Here we caught strange creatures: carp and bullhead and northern and the occasional gar, most of which were unfit to eat but provided action for an energetic and not very patient youngster.

By the time I reached high school, my repertoire had expanded: Dad and I would, mostly by accident, occasionally catch a northern or bass, and I still remember that sudden heavy throb that still gets my heart beating in response. In summer YMCA camp, I swapped around for tackle, and ended up catching bass intentionally on Sturgeon Lake. Among my favorites then—the 1940s, this was—were the Silver Minnow with a pork rind, still a deadly bass-getter in the weeds; and a spotted orange Flatfish, which had more hooks on it than many a tackle box. The bass loved it, and couldn't avoid getting hooked. I also was snagged from the first crashing "take" on a surface lure. From then on there was no turning back; but there was a considerable hiatus.

My teen years were the usual mess: my dad was a teacher, to make things worse, and I had, of course, become a thorough pain in the ass. We went fishing together very little in those years—we had trouble even talking, as I recall—and I'm sure it was a relief when I went off to college. Surprisingly, some of my friends from high school suddenly became more serious about fishing, instead of raising hell, and I gladly joined them.

 # Up North

THE FISHING DID NOT EXCLUDE RAISING HELL. Trips to the north country were often into-the-night marathons, after gathering gear, boats, people, and beer. Friends of friends from other suburbs often joined our junkets, and by the time we raced from South St. Paul to Anoka or Edina or Columbia Heights, it was already late. Finally aimed north on 169, the beer cans would pop (often warm by now), and we'd try to make up the time by flooring it all the way. Not a pretty sporting sight, but we were serious about the fishing.

This fishing was usually after big northern pike. Our favorite spot for several trips was Northern Light Lake, which is just a portage off big Lake Saganaga on the Boundary Waters between Minnesota and Canada, and at the end of the Gunflint Trail. That was, in the mid-1950s, at least a four-hour drive, so we'd crash at a motel somewhere north of Duluth, and swear to be up the Trail at the crack of dawn. We often made it by noon, and were on the water sometime mid-afternoon.

A word about fishing the Boundary Waters then and now. Much remains the same, but several things have changed, almost all of them for the better. We left the landing on Saganaga in a fishing boat with a fifteen-horse Johnson hanging on the back, and roared up the "inner passage" toward a rail portage into Northern Light. We carried heavy canvas tents, food for a platoon, and beer for a brigade. At that time there was a donkey engine that pulled the boat up to the crest of the portage, where it then rolled into Northern Light; there was no way we could have carried everything we brought along.

Because we always got started late, we were usually searching for a camp site about twilight. After a few trips, we could head right for a preferred island site, but some of the early trips were adventures in cruising dark shores that all looked the same until we found anything that looked like we could put a tent on it. There were then, as now, many "established" sites, but fishermen also often just picked a flat place, usually a rock shelf, and set up camp. One of the few advantages to the "good old days" was that there were always lots of spaces available; we seldom saw another boat back on Northern Light, and only once met with a Canadian game warden. That has changed greatly since, and although I'm glad that more people are enjoying the Boundary Waters, and that the rules have changed radically to protect that treasured area, I also liked the real sense of isolation and the freedom of those early days, but then I was nowhere near being a "contemplative man" then (if ever), and for young men from the city it was all a great adventure.

•••

As you can imagine, all of this flailing around by nineteen- and twenty-year-olds made for some messy scenes. There was the night, after a typically late arrival and some later beer and lie-swapping, that we were awakened by a monsoon of a rainstorm, not just startled by the thunder and thud of rain, but nearly swept away by the flood that swept through our ill-planned camp site, turning sleeping bags, tents, equipment and us into a soggy mass, everything hurriedly tied down so it wouldn't wash away. Sleep was done, and by morning we could only survey the wreckage through bleary eyes, and try to straighten things out enough for breakfast—as the rain continued, and continued, for the rest of the day. As city boys, we had lots to learn about wilderness campsites, and drainage, and tying tents down solidly.

My regular partner on these trips was Mike Gebhart, an old neighbor and friend who was then studying at the University of Minnesota. He has since become a highly successful architect on the East Coast, and has long left the Minnesota wilderness behind, but I'm sure he will remember one trip he and I took to Northern Light. We arrived late, as usual, but knew exactly where we were going: a nice established island campsite (islands are preferred as they seldom shelter bear as well as fishermen), the drainage was perfect, there was no rain in sight, although it was windy, and all we had to do was throw up our tent and settle in. We each took a load of gear, and in fifteen minutes had a comfy camp set up, and then went back to the boat for the rest of the equipment. The boat! It was a slightly darker spot out on the dark water, drifting gently away from us in the breeze. We looked at each other, but there was nobody to blame: neither of us had thought to haul the boat further up, or tie it off, and a little wind had been all that was needed.

We looked at each other a little longer, without a word. Finally I started peeling off shoes and pants, and Mike waited me out. "I'll get a fire going," was his only contribution, as I recall.

This was not Lake Superior, after all, where the water was so cold you'd die in minutes; but it was a deep, cold northern lake, and the boat was getting further away by the second. I'm a fairly good swimmer, but it took me a long half-hour to catch up, and by then I was so cold I could just crawl into the ship. Luckily the motor kicked off easily, but shivering in the breeze, made it back to where a nice fire welcomed me. "We were lucky," I said, "but next time, Mike, you get to swim."

There were other hazards, of course. We never did have bear problems, although we certainly left messy enough camps. We did have black flies, no-see-ums, and mosquitoes by the squadron, and always reeked of the oily stuff that passed back then for mosquito repellent. And rain: once a storm settles in the Boundary Waters, it can go on and on for days, and even in a "good" camp, everything eventually gets wet, and smelly, and there's nothing to do.

So we went fishing. We fished in the middle of lightning storms, sitting in a metal boat on open water with the rain slowly filling the boat. We fished when the waves lifted the motor out of the water. Whatever our failures as campers, we were serious fishermen, and it probably kept us from being at each other's throats on bad-weather days without end.

For all the impedimenta we brought along, our fishing gear was quite simple and straightforward: heavy-duty rods with casting reels, usually with an adjustable drag. I don't remember if spinning reels were even around then, but there were none in our arsenals. For lures, each of us had at least a dozen Daredevles, or red-and-white imitations. Why we ended up with just those, I also don't remember. We may have tried other things, but the spoons always worked.

Northern Light has a nice variety of fishlife, with some good walleye and bass as well as panfish. We ignored them all. What we were after were the lunker northern that swarmed in all corners of the lake. Best were small bays, ringed with weeds, and we would troll in one side and around, two or three lines out always, and almost always we'd get at least one good fish, sometimes several. Now these were not record fish, but we could count on a number in the ten- to fifteen-pound category, and a pike that size is probably a better fighter than a twenty-pounder. We lost some in the weeds, of course, and some just to clumsy handling, but we always caught fish, and then went looking for more. The action was almost non-stop: Northern pike are not fussy fish, and seem hungry at all times and in all weather, so we often fished eight or ten hours a day.

Pike are also, to my taste, not great eating fish, but we did take some home each trip. That may have been more for bragging rights than for meat, but for a couple of years I did eat lots of northern.

 # SUPREME TACKLE—A REFLECTION ON GEAR

W HEN I WAS A KID, MY FIRST ROD was a steel pole and my first reel from Montgomery Wards. It had Bakelite sides, no level wind, but it held line. I loaded it with thirty-pound braided line (the only kind, then) and was ready for anything. It was fine for bobber fishing, trolling, and even casting, although there was also no antibacklash; my thumb was what kept it from incredible snarls, once I'd learned just the right pressure to apply, and after I'd untangled dozens of those real bird-nest tangles.

One day when I was ten or twelve, my dad took a friend and me fishing at a local lake. Now my dad's tackle was a little better than mine: the rod was still metal—that was standard—but it had agate-lined guides, and, being longer, had more action than mine. His reel was an inexpensive Shakespeare—nothing fancy, but it did have level wind, and was all solid metal. All in all, though, I wasn't especially envious: my dad wasn't a good caster anyway, but we didn't have to throw far anyway. Bobber fishing only required getting ten feet away from the boat, and the few times we cast to lilly pads for bass, we ran the boat almost into them before throwing plugs; the few feet of distance he could make were unimportant.

My young school friend, on the other hand, had bor-rowed his dad's tackle. I was feeling pretty superior because I had my own stuff, but then I saw what he was using, and there began those first stirrings of tackle acquisitiveness that never seem to leave us who chase fish of any kind.

His rod wasn't any great shakes. This was still before the days of fiberglass, carbon fiber, and the other wonderful stuff that made a rod something alive in your hands, tingling to whip that lure out, out, out beyond all belief and probably all need. But it was obviously better made than my dad's, and certainly than mine: the tip was slender, and the grip actually had pearl handles! (I've never seen this since, except on those old high-end Shakespeare's.) That rod, with a big Flatfish on it, would bend way back on the backcast, then snap forward, hurling the plug incredible distances. I began to see the possibilities in improved equipment right at that point, when he landed a cast on the edge of lily pads far out of my range.

The rod, though, was not the thing that set my fingers tingling. Attached to it was something I'd only seen in store windows, at a distance: a Pflueger Supreme, the masterpiece of reel-building in the 1940s. It was not flashy, but had that understated elegance of the very best and the very expensive. It was in fact a gun-metal grey, but solid and heavy as a fine watch. Like a watch, it had jeweled bearings, a silk-smooth level wind, and an anti-backlash adjustment to avoid the thumb-burnings of lesser reels.

There were other reels made at the time that were probably better, fancy devices crafted for the favored few and the professional sportsman, but this was the top of the line for the dedicated amateur angler. And for the best, of course you had to pay the price.

It's hard to even compare prices these days, but my reel probably cost something like two or three bucks; my dad's maybe five, tops. That dull-gray jewel that I immediately coveted was about twenty-five dollars, an incredible sum for any sporting goods in that day. By comparison, my first .22 rifle, a bolt-action Mossberg 46B with hunting and target sights, a nineteen-shot magazine and wood stock, cost $21.95 at Wards, and that was five or six years later.

Needless to say I didn't even bother asking for a Supreme then. There was a bicycle I really needed, and smaller essential odds and ends that were critical to a twelve-year-old, but that didn't stop me from the impossible dream, and I thought of the long, smooth casts I could make for the next couple of years—in fact, for the next fifty years.

In the meantime, lots of things changed in the angling world (and for me, of course). Rods made of all variations of fiberglass came on the market, and spinning reels, both open-faced and closed. I remember getting my first Mitchell 300, and finding a whole new world of fishing possibilities. I still use it, by the way. Like the M-1 rifle, it is practically indestructible and elegantly simple. It casts, in my opinion, far better than a closed-face reel, and although I use both, it's still my bread-and-butter, all-purpose reel.

More recently, the casting reel has made a dramatic comeback, with sleek polished bodies and silky-smooth work-ings. I also have several of those, and they are indeed finely made machines. To match them, I also had to buy a new rod or two, and as I started using them again, after many years of spinning gear, I began to wonder how they would compare to the old Supreme, always my ideal of the perfect reel.

One day in a flea market, I was browsing a display of fish-ing tackle, and there was the glint of that distinctive grey casing. It looked in good shape, and I bought it without a second thought. And within a few months, when I'd actually started looking for them, I found another in a garage sale, and several on eBay. There are a surprising number still around, because like the 8N Ford tractor or Model 12 Winchester, they never seem to wear out. My second one was the fancy model with a star drag, a relatively heavy-duty piece of equipment. Both were pristine in appearance, and to my surprise when I spun the handles each still turned effortlessly, frictionlessly, if there's such a word.

When I tried them out using the new rods I'd bought for today's best technology, I found they would not quite give me the same distance, but they felt so good! They also gave me just as great accuracy, which is really more important: how often do you really have to cast tremendous distances, when you're fishing around a patch of lily pads or on the edge of a drop-off?

I admit it: the brand-new reels are gathering dust in my tackle collection somewhere, and I'm finally using what, to me, is still the ultimate fishing reel. After all, these old beauties have been around for upwards of half a century and show almost no signs of wear, and I have no guarantee that those brand-new plastic and aluminum space-age versions will hold up anywhere near as well. And the cost? Well, the new reels I admit were not top-of-the-line, but they still ran well over fifty dollars apiece. The Supremes, after a little haggling, each cost twenty-five dollars, but then, that's exactly what their price should be.

10,000 LAKES

PPR: BUT AS I WAS SAYING, Minnesota was the ideal birthplace for a prospective fisherman, and I was introduced to the waters and wiles of the state almost *in ovum*, when I waded into Lake Owasso and almost joined the fishes. I think since then much of my life has been spent simply wading deeper and deeper into the homes of bass, trout, and sailfish, trying to learn, if not to breathe like them, at least to think like them. That, as I was trying to tell you earlier, is why I am qualified to write about fishing.

Reader: Okay, I'm semi-convinced. I even read the first few pages last night—when I could have been fishing—and I'm convinced you are actually a fisherman. I'll even excuse the fact that you're a professor and are going to finally get to the good stuff only after a preoration, argument, and lots of windy speeches along the way. Just try to hurry it up, and get to the trout as soon as possible. I plan to go fishing tonight, whether you've given me any useful advice or not.

PPR: Fair enough. In the meantime, like my honored ancestor, I'm going to speak of the lesser fishes, and of the experiences that prepared me for my later encounters with trout.

Yes, Minnesota is a fisherman's paradise. Every year one and a half million of us pay the state a minimal fee to wander over more water than anyone has a right to, and catch fairly generous limits of everything from panfish to bass, pike, muskie, sturgeon, trout, salmon, and yes, walleyed pike, the regional favorite. Now I must admit being a heretic: I'm not crazy about walleye fishing. Yes, they taste wonderful, and they're a beautiful fish, but they don't live up to their looks in fighting ability, nor in the way their caught.

Now this mattered to me from the first time a large-mouth crashed to the surface to nail my waddling Flatfish, and it became almost a mystical experience to me later, when I began casting to trout with dry flies. Back in Minnesota after two long periods of living in the Southwest, I did my duty, and went wall-eye fishing. This usually involved sitting in the middle of a deep lake, wrapped in the traditional ten layers of wool and wind-proofing, guaranteed to sink you directly to the bottom—which didn't matter, because hypothermia would undoubtedly do you in before touching down. And to be sure that we would some-time swamp our small craft, walleye fishing must be done when there's a "chop," that is, when it's windy, which also means cold, and often even includes snow if you're out for the grand "opener" of the season.

Well, I didn't do that much. It's a little like duck hunting, which seems to appeal to the Norwegian temperament in Min-nesotans: you really have to suffer for your sport, and anything like pleasure in the outdoors means you're not really enjoying yourself. That and the fact that landing a walleye is about as exciting as winching in a log kept me from ever being a committed walleye man. I would catch one, almost by accident, when trolling or fish-ing one of the local rivers, and I was always pleased. They are ex-cellent eating, after all. However, I really preferred almost any of the other options that the state waters offered.

In the springtime particularly, crappie fishing is both pro-ductive and fun; at least you're usually keeping the bait moving, even if it's a minnow, and a good big slab-sided crappie can be explosive on a light rod. Similarly, sunfish, especially during the early spring spawn, can offer non-stop action. They're so prolific in our southern Minnesota lakes that the problem often is just keeping the little ones off your hook until you can pick up some decent "keepers." Using a fly rod and poppers, flies, or sinking lures really made it sporty, and because they were in close to the weeds early on, you could wade in and hook an endless number in three or four feet of water. Sunfish have a kind of spicy taste, to me; a real richness that makes catching and cleaning a mess of them a pleasure.

This should be enough for anyone. Minnesota is a giant fish cauldron, really, and if you're out for a meal or just an evening's good sport, you can keep fully occupied all through the few sunlit months we're allowed in our none-so-gentle northern clime. And then you can go on, of course. I'll come to that uniquely northern madness later on.

However, I wanted more action, and I'd already found bass the most exciting kind of water show I could get. Besides, I think bass are very tasty, unlike many natives who scorn them as only a sport fish and not worth the keeping. Done properly, a few nice bass filets are, to my taste, just about as good as walleye or sunfish, and certainly several steps above northern pike.

I started getting serious with bass in the lakes around Mankato, Minnesota, where I taught at the state university. Now these are not your clear, deep, cold northern lakes, cradled in the great rock slab that overlies the upper third of the state. Here lakes are depressions in the rich black earth of farm country; the bottoms are mud, and weeds are prolific. Nonetheless, they're teeming with life, including everything fishy from bullheads to bass, and since bass are considered second-class by our walleye majority, lots of them grow to a ripe, fat maturity.

The larger lakes in this area, and for that matter every-where, are well used. Every usable inch of shoreline has its cabin or full-time home, and every home its boat. That means lots of traffic, from the nasty little personal watercraft to roaring airboats, pontoons to water skiers. It's still possible to find the quiet bay, and I've had some good fishing in the little backwaters to the background of roaring motors, but the better settings and some of the best fishing are in smaller waters.

My boat is a joke by the modern standards that require 150 horse power and coolers, captain's chairs, steering wheels, and electronic depth finders, fish finders, and cameras. It's a twelve-foot aluminum Smokercraft, inherited from my father-in-law twenty-five years ago; he bought it another twenty years before that, and it was second-hand then! It's dented, but it's sturdy, doesn't leak, and is so light, I can carry it on top of my truck, if I want. A few years back, though, I built a trailer for it, so I needn't unload it every trip. It's powered by a two-horse Johnson and a trolling motor. The only equipment is a set of rodracks that will hold four or five bass sticks, and it's ready to go any time I get the urge.

When I do, I head for one of those smaller lakes; there are a half-dozen in the area, and they're pretty much alike. They too have been built up, but the boating is more limited. Often there'll be only a few pontoons or smallish boats drifting around, and only rarely have I had to compete with other fishermen in my favorite spots. Because these are shallow lakes, they weed up early in the summer. My little ship is perfect for slipping through the weedbeds along the shoreline, and that's usually where the fishing is best.

It's not always best—sometimes it's not even good—as bass are as moody as trout. There have been evenings of pounding the water with Rapalas, poppers, Flatfish, spinner baits, and eveything else possible, and not a single fish would respond. That's rare, fortunately. There are usually at least a few young, eager fish who'll hit anything, so even if we have no braggin' stringer, we're not skunked. And there are a few nights, like the one my son Hugh and I experienced on little Reed's Lake.

We had gotten to the lake about 6:30, and crossed to the north end where the weedbeds made for the best fishing, if the hardest. Surface baits, by the way, are the only possibility after the first few weeks of the season in these small lakes; the weeds cover perhaps two-thirds of the surface, and in the open spaces where you can drop a lure, the water is only a few feet deep. Now one of my theories about bass is that the really good fishing almost never starts before 8:00. Like most fishing theories, it doesn't always hold true, but more than most, it has worked out. However, we were on the fishing beds by seven, and of course started casting right away. And right away we began catching fish. My son's first cast brought a nice two-pounder boiling to the surface. Before he'd landed it, I was hooked into a slightly larger fish.

So it went. We caught fish on about half our casts, and soon lost track of how many we actually landed and released. Our stringer was full of hefty largemouth up to four pounds, and we actually quit before full dark—something I have real trouble doing—literally tired out from hooking and playing fish.

We didn't land them all. The hazard of this kind of fishing is again the weeds, which the fish make for as soon as they're hooked. Once they're tangled up, they often get enough leverage to break loose, or sometimes you simply lose line, lure and fish. Even the boat can get bogged down in the weedbeds. Motors just won't go through them, even with weedless props, and we spend lots of time and energy rowing or poling through weed masses to get to the edge of open water.

It's a messy and often frustrating kind of fishing, but it pays off in many ways besides the occasional meal of bass fillets. These small backwaters are full of wildlife, and most evenings the birds are in full voice: ducks sound off overhead, and pheasant and smaller birds croak or warble from the marsh. Water birds make their final passes overhead before settling in for the night, and we've even had a pair of trumpeter swans drift curiously right up to our boat. And on a clear night, the sudden explosion around a Rapala on the glassy surface is always a "peak moment." Is he any size? Can I keep him out of the weeds? And will there be more, later on.

THE OTHER
9,000 LAKES

F OR MANY YEARS BASS WERE MY PASSION, although I had no
interest in the kind of competitive, mechanized frenzy that is
"serious" bass fishing. I just wanted to catch a few nice fish on
lakes that were relatively quiet, and on the simplest of terms. Inevitably any fisherman collects tackle—the latest wonder lure, a
few "extra" rods and reels, knives, scales, pliers, and disgorgers,
and so on, and eventually larger and larger tackle boxes. But I
drew the line at depth finders and fish finders and cameras.
Somehow they just didn't fit my idea of fishing, nor did a bigger
boat and motor. I liked being a little closer to the surface, as if I
were a not-too-foreign object in the water, and only a little bigger version of what I was hunting. So I still fish from my little
Smokercraft, and although my tackle box is jammed with lures
from the last sixty years, nothing basic has changed.

Fishing southern Minnesota bass has its limitations,
though, and is a pretty down-and-dirty, labor-intensive struggle.
After the first month of the season, the weeds have made fishing
most good shorelines almost impossible, and even running a
motor through some of the lakes a challenge.

As you move north of the Twin Cities, however, the nature of Minnesota lakes begins to change. The rock-bound lakes
of the far north, where I'd fished for pike as a young man, were
equally good for bass, and by this time I had two new fishing
partners.

My sons Owen and Hugh were twelve and ten when we
took our first trip together into the north country. We left from

Ely, the classic jumping-off place for much of the canoe country, and portaged in to Bass Lake, a place I'd visited once before with a friend from Grand Rapids. He knew the lake well, and it was only a mile hike from a parking space just a few miles north of Ely. On this trip we (I) carried a canoe, a much lighter, smaller tent, and everything else we needed in a couple of backpacks. Still, it was a pretty good load for one adult and two youngsters, and it wasn't made any lighter when I missed the trail from car to lake. There is nothing more frustrating than wandering through the pine woods with a canoe over your head, occupying both hands, and mosquitoes and black flies working their will on you, except realizing you are also lost—and that you have two trusting children trailing along on your errant path.

We wandered for an infinity, the boys groaning like good soldiers about the weight of their loads, but really enjoying the adventure, and I peering out from the gunwales for any sign of Bass Lake. When, eventually, I saw a clear space ahead, suggesting a thinning of trees toward water, I really had no idea if it was Bass Lake or no. In that country, you can't really walk very far without hitting water.

At the edge of the woods, the land dropped sharply to lake shore. We tied a rope to the canoe and slid it down, then followed, sliding and stumbling, to a rocky promontory. And there, thank whatever gods may be, was a familiar island with just the outline of a campground my friend and I had used on the first trip.

It was just getting dark when we landed the canoe, and the first order of business, after throwing the tent up, was to feed two starving boys. Now Owen had started in Boy Scouts, and I let him set up the kitchen—a campfire and rusty grill, even though we had a small cooking stove with us—and we made huge hamburgers, which barely were given time to warm up before being devoured. It was not a standard camp fare, but I'd thought the first night ought to be special. There were plenty of canned goods for the rest of the stay.

And of course we had to stay up late, that first night, although we'd all had plenty of exercise. We set up the rest of the camp, stumbling around with flashlights, the boys scaring each other with shadows in the pine woods, and then really turning big-eyed as a pair of loons began a maniacal symphony. I've never heard them really turn it on. We tend to think of just the one haunting call, but they have a real repertoire. All of it is a little eerie, but also very beautiful, and we sat up by the fire until after 11:00, listening to the music, and the silence, of the north woods.

The weather was crisp—this was still early June—but perfect. We had no serious rain in the three days on Bass Lake, and we fished and explored at our will. The boys had already done some fishing around home, but it had been mainly for panfish— lots of action to keep them interested, and some good eating when it was over. This was different, and I wasn't sure how they'd react to hours of casting. Fortunately, we began hooking fish right away, using copper spoons and medium-running plugs. We were really bass fishing, but there were also plenty of northern to keep the action going. In one spot, over a sunken island, we hooked six or seven bass, some in the two-pound range. Then along the rocky shore, Owen hooked a really good fish, got it up to the boat—and I lost it, trying to bring it in. If there's anything Oedipal in our relationship, I know exactly where it began.

What I really hoped to give them, besides fish, was a taste of what the real outdoors was like, in a rather tame version. Our campsite even had a privy on it, and we weren't at all far from civilization in other ways—our car was a mile away, at least in a straight line, and Ely was just down the road. Still, if it wasn't the forest primeval, it was still relatively wild. The loggers hadn't gotten this far yet, and because it wasn't a walleye lake there were no other fishermen the three days we stayed. And it was beautiful. We were just on the edge of the Laurentian Shield, and the shoreline was solid rock, with deep clear water gathered in its bowl. Besides the loons (and the mosquitoes), there were beaver dams and plenty of water birds, as well as the usual small woods-dwellers and singers. At night, playing fiddle to the loons, the pines whispered in the breeze, and lent their rich tangy smell to the air. Most of all, there was space: no people, no rules, lots of new things to explore—very different from the flat black farm-land of our home place.

A friend and colleague, Richard Terrill, has written about the inevitable loss of wilderness in our lives, and what it will mean. We and my sons may be the last generations to have any real experience with these sacred places; an exploding population and our general destructiveness and waste will probably overrun these small islands of the natural world that still remain. I wanted to be sure my sons would at least be among those who knew something of what we will lose, and to fight against the going, even if is in inevitable.

When we left Bass Lake, I knew it better than the first time, and for that matter, I'd spotted the portage very soon after we arrived, so the trip back to the car was an easy hike. We'd eaten a few bass fresh from the water, and took out only a few filets; most went back to become the big ones we'd catch (and maybe lose) sometime later on, or maybe when one or both of the boys would return years from now. That night we celebrated our return to civilization with pizza and showers in an Ely motel, and by the next night we were back in Mankato. It's a small town, but for a few days it seemed far too noisy and overcrowded. It was the real world, of course, and a still somewhat insulated part of it, but it's the future, only worse.

I don't know what lasting effect that and other trips will have on my sons, but I hope they'll return to the wilderness. And I hope too they will become fishermen, because that will take them into places where humans are not the only species. At the very least I hope they'll remember it, and the smell and sound of pines and lapping water, the music of the loons, and the lazy drift of a canoe in a clear cold lake. I do know that they talk about it, even now, years later, and just after we returned I overheard them describing their adventure to their friends, including the part about, "We got really lost on the way in, and Dad couldn't find the lake for a long time." And I thought I'd gotten away with it!

PPR and Reader,
Again

Reader: So now you're going to tell me how not to take a fishing trip? I thought I was supposed to learn something useful from this book. And where are the trout, Mr. Piscator?

PPR: Sometimes, gentle sir, the best advice comes from the worst experience, and all the "how-to" tales will only prepare you for a world where everything goes perfectly. This brief account deals with the pitfalls to avoid in the real world, and is, therefore, the perfect morality tale. It demonstrates how the sins of hubris and arrogance can bring even the mighty to their knees, weeping and wailing, and . . .

Reader: Hey, come on! These are only fishing stories, right? Let's not get all religious and philosophical over a few northern pike. And speaking of that, again, I'm mostly interested in trout, so I want some advice like Izaac Walton would give me.

PPR: When we speak of Walton's Piscator, remember he is the Compleat Angler, and not a trout purist. So in his footsteps I am pleased to include the lesser fishes (although I'm not so keen on chub as he was) before addressing the glories and mysteries of that king of watery creatures. This modesty should be part of the true fisherman's demeanor, as should be his reverence before the natural world. It is inevitable that the solitary sport should lend itself to contemplation, to how the world is reflected in that glittering stream or lake, and what one's own role is in that world.

Reader: Look, I just want to catch a few fish, especially trout, and have a good time doing it. As long as I've already bought the book, I'll try another chapter, but I hope I get more advice than just using copper spoons, and I hope we get a trout in here soon.

PPR: If it's pleasure you seek in your quest for fishing—and it should be—believe me, this chapter will be most instructive, and then shortly we will get to the trout, as I did in my own quest.

Reader: Okay, but I'm beginning to wish I'd bought that Norman MacLean instead.

THE INCOMPLETE
ANGLER

As MUCH AS WE MINNESOTANS LOVE our state, if we're fishermen we recognize that the best fishing is always "up north," and inevitably this means the further north one goes, the better it should be, and this, also inevitably, leads us to Canada. Whether this is true or no, it is obvious that Minnesota lakes are crowded with fishermen; even the Boundary Waters are no longer places to find solitude, as they were when Anne and I, and later my sons and I traveled there. The rules for using the lakes are an improvement, but they're only a stopgap intended to lessen the damage that will inevitably come from more and more visitors to this controlled wilderness, and the fishing will also suffer.

That was the thinking that sent me and two colleagues from Mankato State University up beyond the border into Ontario lakes several times. John Otis was an English professor as well, and also a Navy Reserve pilot, so on occasion we flew from his place in Grand Rapids to the more isolated lakes of Canada. Jack Lawson, an English/Philosophy professor, was a veteran of the outdoors, a hiker and camper for many years, and we all knew something about the wilderness.

However, our first trip in search of more pristine waters was a disaster. It wasn't our ignorance of the outdoors, but that we simply ignored, in our pride, some of the basics.

It seemed simple enough: we had picked the region we wanted to fish, and left ourselves some options. There was a decent road from Ignace to the Pickle Lake region, which we'd been told was not overused, but had several lodges and outfitters along the way. We would drive up, this first time, since landing sites were uncertain for the plane, and try to arrange a charter fly-in near the terminus of the road. That failing, we could fish from one of the lodges along the way. The fly-in was our preference, because it would take us into quite remote territory where the fishing should be best.

That was about the extent of our planning. We'd meet at John's cabin in Grand Rapids in early September, with Jack driving up from Mankato. I'd be coming in from the Stratford, Ontario, Shakespeare Festival, going from one kind of Canada to another in a few days. Anne and I were camping, so I had my gear along. In fact, the first complication we encountered was that all of us had our gear, far too much to take along. Our first task in Grand Rapids was sorting out duplications and triplications of tents, cooking utensils, food, and camp tools into a manageable kit that we could stow in a light airplane and then pack in a boat.

We finally had my Ford van packed with just the essentials, and were at the International Falls customs by ten in the morning. Our first upset occurred here, in the form of a young lady who informed us cheerfully that no fire permits were being issued, and that there was a good chance we would not even be allowed a camping permit in Ontario because of the very dry condition of the woods. To actually request our permits, we would have to stop at the Ontario Forestry Centre, and we approached that office with sinking hearts. Fortunately, the agent there was able to issue us a permit for travel and camping at least, as she said the authorities were still arguing about whether or not to close the area completely.

We grabbed our precious paperwork and headed rapidly for Ignace, 350 miles away. We arrived just before dark, and decided to start up Highway 599 to Pickle Lake since there would certainly be plenty of pull-off areas in the wilderness further north. By 9:00, all of us were exhausted. We'd passed a few likely looking spots earlier, but in the rush to get up the road we'd continued driving until we couldn't see any pull-offs, if they were there. Finally, just ten miles short of Savant Lake, the one town on the road, we stopped at a lodge and paid two dollars to camp on their grounds.

The next day our lack of planning really began to show up. We stopped in Savant Lake to get some information there about conditions further up the road. We were told, a) there were no flying services further north, b) there was an airline in Pickle Lake, but no boats or motors available there, and c) there was a regular, well-established fly-in outfitter in Pickle! Since Savant Lakers seemed to know about as much as we did about their neighbors 100 miles away, we decided to call Pickle Lake (there was a charter service there, according to the general store owner who seemed the most reliable informant, and also owned the telephone.

We had not counted, however, on the Savant-Pickle Lake telephone service. It took almost two hours to get a line to the charter service. Their rates seemed okay, and they could take us in, but by that time it was almost 11:00. We decided to try two of the lodges on the way north—most of the rest were already closed for the season—and if we could get a boat and motor we'd fish that day in one of the lakes along the road. If we had no luck, we would drive on through to Pickle and fly back in late afternoon. I have never been sure how much of that message got through. I'm certain we didn't get all the information we needed, probably because we didn't ask and because the connection kept breaking up.

We were beginning to think our luck had turned when we found the first lodge open for business, but then learned there were only enough boats for the guests and absolutely no motors available. The second place, also open, was even worse. There, the owner (who was definitely not a Chamber of Commerce member) told us that, not only did he have no boats or motors available, but that he didn't bother fishing there himself—he went to Saskatchewan if he wanted to catch anything!

On that note, we decided that, since we'd come this far, we might as well see the end of the road, even if there were no fish at it, and we headed resolutely for Pickle Lake. We finally dragged in mid-afternoon, and found the airlines without much difficult. The only really active businesses in town were a fish processing plant and two air services, whose main business was hauling fish in to the plant and carrying supplies further north to prospectors, geologists, and other wandering souls.

We talked to the office manager and the chief pilot, and arranged for a "minimum trip" to Kapikik Lake, about twenty-five miles west of town, but then we were told that they had no boats back on the lake, since they were not outfitters, and they didn't know if we could find a boat in town or not. Finally they scrounged up an aluminum car-top boat, which they would let us use, but when we asked about a motor, they just shrugged. There were two in town, both owned by private parties, and not for rent. In fact, they had not tried to get oars, which left us with a fairly useless craft. Also, by now the wind had come up, and the lake was too rough to fly from, especially with a boat underneath, and further, since we'd have to carry the boat, a larger and much more expensive plane would be necessary!

By now we had reached that point of despair and exhaustion at which we just accepted each new stroke of bad fortune, and we decided to wait to see if the wind would die down so we could get off early that evening. And to see if we could find some oars. We retired to the local hotel, and after several beers, began to feel better about the whole business. When the pilot came in about six o'clock to tell us he'd found some oars, we were almost ecstatic—but he cooled us down by telling us that it was still too windy to get off that day. We would meet him at the waterfront at 7:00 the next morning. This was the end of our second day, and we had yet to wet a line.

By the time we left to find a campsite just out of town, we were feeling so good about everything (thanks to several more beers) that even discovering we'd lost our axe and had brought none of the several can openers along couldn't dismay us. The next morning we were not quite so jubilant, but we were, with great effort, at the dock by 7:00. By 8:00 we were still at the dock, and for an hour after the pilot arrived, we sulked around while he took care of his more important business. We finally took off a little after 10:00, after loading and waiting for the plane to be gassed (which should have been done the night before). We also discovered, as soon as we were settled, that the plane was primarily a fish-carrier for the processing plant. The smell of old fish was almost overwhelming once we'd closed ourselves in.

I had managed in the long wait to produce another hatchet and a can opener, so when we landed in the middle of Lake Kapikak, we were all set for three lovely days and very eager to leave the fishy ambience of the plane. The pilot couldn't get near shore because of rocks, so we unloaded in the middle of the lake, drifting in toward the point on which we would camp. The boat was loaded and all three of us were settled. I picked up an oar and tried to fit it into the lock—and it was too big! By this time nothing could stop us: we poured cooking oil into the locks, pounded the oars in with the hatchet and ground our way toward shore as the plane taxied out toward the middle of the lake.

Believe it or not, the fishing was wonderful. We caught and released almost 100 northern and walleyes that first day, and things stayed at that pace the next day and Sunday morning as well. There were few really big fish—our largest northern was eleven or twelve pounds—but there was lots of action, our meals were good, and the weather was okay. There were a few incidents: Jack dislocated his shoulder in a fall on the lakeshore, and even though it popped back into place he was in agony most of the time. We still had roughly three times as much food as we needed, and one night the temperature dropped abruptly below freezing, so that we had to move the camp stove into the tent to keep the chill off the sleeping bags. But these were normal hazards, and didn't interfere seriously with our good fishing. On the last day, we began keeping walleyes to take out, and in an hour or so had our limit of eighteen.

Our final inconvenience came at 12:00 Sunday, when we had just pulled into camp to start packing for our return flight at 1:00. No sooner had we stepped ashore than we heard the twin-engine Beechcraft in the distance, and in a few minutes could see him starting his drop into the lake—the first time he'd been early for anything that year, I'm sure. You can't simply keep a plane circling or taxiing, so we broke camp in record time, and when he cut his motors we were throwing the last of our gear into the boat.

The trip back was uneventful, except for the groans and snores of exhaustion from three days of rowing sticking oars, and the anxiety of our "vacation," but at that, we were lucky to have fished at all. Any one of a dozen factors we hadn't taken care of in advance could have turned our trip into a complete fiasco, and though it was a real adventure, with a lot of the unexpected thrown in, our later trips to the far north have been planned down to the last toothpick, and we have all reservations in hand at least a month before we leave.

 # UP NORTH AGAIN

Reader: You've mentioned your wife, only to say she's a tolerant woman. Are you still married, by the way?

PPR: Yes, and happily so.

Reader: Well, you seem to be off on fishing trips a great deal of the time. Also, you probably come home foul and fishy, with grimy clothes and slimy fish. I don't understand why any woman would tolerate that kind of life. Doesn't she get tired of being married to a fisherman?

PPR: Oh, good sir, I've given you the wrong impression of my wife, and my marriage; or rather, of my fishing life and my married life. They are married, so to speak, and Anne not only tolerates my fishing, but has been my partner in much of my fishing forays. I'd be glad to show you how to make marriage and fishing coexist.

Reader: That might actually be useful, because I've only been married a short time, and my fishing has already become a bit of an issue. In fact, she seems a little upset when I disappear for a weekend, or come home late for dinner, or bring home a beautiful stringer of fish for her to prepare. I think it may come down to cutting back on fishing, or finding a new wife.

PPR: Oh, dear sir, I hope it doesn't come to that. Let me give you a few examples of how my marriage and fishing have not only coexisted, but how each has benefited from the other, so that my fishing has been more enjoyable and my marriage better in every way. But first, I must give you an immediate and essential piece of advice: clean your own fish!

Reader: Okay, I can do that. I just saw a nifty electric knife by Rapala that will make fish-cleaning easy. I'll just use the kitchen sink, so I can plop the offal right in the kitchen garbage, and . . .

PPR: Oh, my, you have so much to learn! First, be careful not to buy every fishing tool you see (although that is a wonderful tool, which I'd like to borrow if you still feel compelled to buy it), or at least don't display it blatantly to your bride. New fishing equipment should simply appear, usually months after you've bought it, and you must seem surprised that she's never noticed it before. Also, unless you're quite rich, it's not a good idea to buy a new Sage rod when the house needs repainting—roughly the same cost, probably. Don't let it appear that fishing is eating up the budget; either practice some moderation, or keep new equipment well out of sight until it's aged a bit, and doesn't look new.

Second, the kitchen is hers, unless you plan to do all the cooking. Clean fish outside, or at least in the basement, and only bring the nice clean filets into the kitchen, preferably already wrapped or at least in a basin of water, ready to cook.

Reader: All right, I admit I'm new to both fishing and marriage, and maybe I need a little advice, but you're supposed to be the fishing guru, not a marriage expert. Maybe you ought to stick to your own business, and leave the domestic advice to someone else.

PPR: (Sighing) But, my dear sir, as I said before, the two are inseparable. If you want to be a fisherman, and also stay married, you must learn how to balance the two, else you must either quit fishing or plan on a divorce in the near future.

There are only these few scenarios, and you must choose one early in your marriage. One, you can ignore the fact that you're married, and simply go fishing whenever you wish.

Reader: Well, that's what I've been doing, and my wife is not happy with it at all.

PPR: Good. You've recognized that this approach simply will not work in most cases. If you do choose this, the macho approach, you must have a wife who tolerates anything, or reconcile yourself to a lifetime of bickering, or a bothersome series of divorces, or living singly.

Two, you can cut back on fishing until it's no longer a large part of your life and try other activities that include your wife. This can, for some, be a completely satisfactory solution.

Reader: Hey, no way! I want to be a fisherman, not play bridge or join a book club. Isn't there any way I can have a happy marriage and still fish as much as I want?

PPR: Fortunately, yes, there is a way, but it takes some effort on your part, and some willingness on hers. You can take her along on your fishing trips, but be certain she's comfortable and that you don't simply fish and ignore her. If she shows a real interest in fishing, excellent. She may become your regular partner, and you must not be upset when she outfishes you. My Anne happens to be an outdoor girl, and on our very first trip, to a local river, she caught a beautiful sixteen-pound northern pike—while I caught nothing. I had not learned at that time to let it go, and I came back by myself and fished until I hooked an eighteen-pounder. Fortunately, she didn't resent it, but, looking back, I need not have been so competitive. I was still in macho mode, however, and only beginning to learn how to reconcile fishing and marriage.

As it turned out, she only liked to fish occasionally, and I soon learned I didn't have to outdo her to prove anything. She has since gone along on some of my local junkets, and sometimes not, but she at least knows why I love fishing—and can love her at the same time.

Reader: Oh, that's so sweet (sneeringly). But what about longer trips, say out West for trout. Is it possible to take her on those and not have her bored to death? My wife doesn't fly-fish, and doesn't want to, so how do I keep her happy and still fish all I want?

PPR: My good sir, the trout themselves can resolve that issue, without her being the least interested in fishing for them. It's a truism that trout have the loveliest homes, so you'll be taking her into mountain and river country that will take her breath away. That should be a start. Then you must also make some compromises. Certainly, fish all you want—for one day. Then the next, find something you both can share. Simply explore some of that beautiful country with her, including some of the interesting Western towns. Or, if you're lucky, she'll have some other interests that she wants to do on her own, leaving you free to return to the trout. In our travels, for instance, my wife and I have worked out a very satisfactory compromise (she doesn't fly fish either, by the way). We divide the time, so that for every hour I fish, she gets to go rock-hounding or antiquing. Since I've developed a mild interest in both, sometimes I'll accompany her, but just as often, she'll go off on her own and leave me to the streams.

Reader: All right, maybe some of that will work, but I often camp while on those longer trips, and it can be pretty well, basic. Do you think she'll tolerate that?

PPR: It has been my experience, dear Reader, that women make far better campers than men. I can't answer for your wife, but if she has any appreciation for the beautiful world of trout, she'll enjoy living in it, and camping is the best way to do that. You may also find that your camp will be more home-like, and very probably cleaner, if she shares it with you. And you may also want to try staying in motels occasionally—often very near a desirable trout stream—just to make certain she's comfortable.

Reader: Okay, I'll try some of those things, and then I guess it's up to her. The only way to find out, I suppose, is to take her on a long trip and let her discover my world, and see if she likes it.

PPR: Make it a short trip the first time. Remember, the object is to involve her in the fishing/camping world and at the same time making sure she's comfortable and able to indulge herself, follow her own interests. You don't want to get in the middle of a three-week junket and discover that she hates it and only wants to go home. That may put an end to your marriage as a partnership, and perhaps also an end to either your fishing or your marriage itself. Let me give you an example from my experience of how not to treat your wife if you want her to accept and enjoy the fishing life.

Reader: You're certainly full of bad examples. I'm not sure you're the one to be giving advice, if most of your own experiences have been mistakes.

PPR: Ah, that's just the point. We should learn more from our errors than our successes, and avoid them in the future, and you can profit from my experience by never getting into similar situations. So do you want to hear the story?

Reader: Do I have a choice?

PPR: Certainly. You can simply turn the page, and shut me up for as long as you want. That's one of the nice things about books, and another reason for buying this volume. However, I sincerely hope you'll read of my misadventure for your own benefit, and for the happy blending of your marriage and fishing.

I had been married only a short time when I invited my wife to join me on an adventure into the Boundary Waters Canoe area.

It was an area I knew well, as I've described earlier in the book. Those trips were the rough-and-ready outings of fishing enthusiasts, caring little for the conditions under which we traveled and fished, as long as we caught big pike and had enough beer.

Now I was still a bit uncertain about traveling with a woman as my companion, but I had learned just enough to know that the old fish-'til-you drop approach needed some adjustments. First, we had ten days for the trip, so there was plenty of time to prepare our equipment, and we could go at a leisurely pace, enjoying the trip in to Northern Light taking our time about setting up a comfortable camp. Also, we'd fish less obsessively and only under comfortable conditions, take some time to prepare proper meals, and leave plenty of time for reading, exploring the area, and just getting to know each other.

And it actually went as planned, for the most part. It was a pleasure to motor slowly up the beautiful calm waters of Saganaga, taking in the spectacular scenery for a change instead of roaring past it. We also took more time with the portages, partly to get a better look at these rough paths through the wilderness, and also because we had more equipment to carry. This was my own doing, because I'd decided that my new bride was going to be as comfortable as possible, and thereby learn to love the wilderness as I did, and also enjoy the experience of traveling and living in it. To that end, we had added considerably to the equipment list. There were still plenty of Daredevils, and some beer, along with tents and food, but we also packed cots, air mattresses, and sleeping bags, more clothing than the single pants and shirt that had been my uniform on earlier trips, a gasoline-fueled Coleman stove and actual cooking equipment, instead of one fry pan and a pot, as well as an assortment of food and drink, and of course more toilet articles: a razor and shaving cream, new to my camp experience, washcloths and towels and soap and myriad other articles designed to keep us reasonably clean and presentable. We were still at the early stage of marriage where each day was a little like a first date, and one was not ready to reveal the little flaws and blemishes that would inevitably be revealed with the greater familiarity of a long marriage.

Surprisingly, everything went perfectly—the weather was delightful, warm enough in the daytime and cool at night, and we had no significant rain. Our camp was on one of those granite outcroppings, where we could soak in the sun, yet also just on the edge of a stand of delicious-smelling pine for privacy, and one edge was shallow enough to beach the canoe easily. We actually took time for some hikes and sightseeing, so the fishing was only one activity and not an obsession, and our meals were, if not gourmet fare, at least far better than the beans-and-weenies of my earlier trips. Each meal was actually planned in advance, with something different for each of the ten days.

It was idyllic indeed—until the day we left. We woke to a heavy downpour, and rather than attempt to cook our last rather lavish breakfast, we settled for coffee and a hasty packing-up of already soaked equipment. That should not have ruined everything. It almost always rains at some time during a canoe-country trip, and we had plenty of raingear among our provisions. Unfortunately, because of the unusually heavy load of equipment, the canoe rode sluggishly, even with the little five-horse motor pushing it along, and the portages were increasingly difficult: more trips with the now-soaked equipment, and treacherous, slippery trails that left us mud-covered and mosquito-bitten after just the first couple of hours.

Even that was endurable, but the real trouble was yet to come, when we reached the last stretch of open water before entering Big Saganaga Lake, with a ten-mile run still ahead of us. By now the storm had worked itself into a fury. The little bay we had to cross was white-capped, and what we could see of Saganaga was a maelstrom: huge waves, with sheets of rain lashing their foaming tops, and a greenish cast to the sky that suggested worse to come.

Nonetheless, we started across the bay. Our canoe was now sloshing with rainwater, and riding perilously low, and just as we pushed off, the motor gave a last shudder and stopped.

I quickly grabbed a paddle and put us back on the shore we'd just left, where we huddled in the open as I examined the motor. The problem was simple: the screws holding the engine and prop shaft together had vibrated loose and dropped out, so the outboard was essentially in two separate parts, and of course impossible to operate. It took another hour to fashion makeshift screws from oval sinkers and twist them into the four holes as tightly as they would go. The motor would run, but I had little confidence in the makeshift repairs. However, by now my bride was soaking wet, her hair in tangles and red-and-runny nosed, so I decided to push on. Bad move! The bay had built up some serious rollers by now, and we had to cross it to reach a small island just on the edge of Saganaga.

We started across, the motor sputtering ominously while I tried to hold the canoe head-on into the waves, and even at that angle the spray from the prow drenched us further with icy-cold water, and then contributed to the mess sloshing around the bottom of the craft. We had put on everything warm and woolen that we owned under the rain-gear and, had we tipped at that point, would have sunk like rocks in the deep glacial lake.

After at least a month, our craft bumped the shore of the island, and only then I noticed that Anne's hands were stone-white and clamped like claws to the gunnels of our floundering canoe; she could or would not even move until I had jumped into knee-deep water and dragged the heavy craft well up on the beach.

And that was far from the end. Saganaga was impossible, so we set up a makeshift, drenched camp on the one small piece of open land available. Gone were all the amenities, either packed away deep in the duffle bags, or if reachable, so wet as to be unusable.

Also, our very careful dietary planning became a liability: we had planned each meal—for ten days, and now the ten days were up and there was almost nothing left. That evening we ate the remains of the morning's elegant breakfast, and then huddled around a sputtering fire under awning of our sagging tent.

After a miserable night's sleep, I was up early, attempting to catch breakfast—and perhaps lunch and dinner as well. Now we had had two or three excellent fish dinners, one of walleye fillets in breadcrumbs and another of platters of delicate sunfish. Oh, and one full-size bass, one of my personal favorites, and plentiful back on Northern Light.

I did catch fish on our island too: northern pike, one after another, and nothing else at all. I'll eat northern when I'm desperate, and we certainly were now. We gnawed on them straight off cooking sticks, like pickerel shish-kabobs. All our cooking gear was somewhere in the jumble on the bottom of the boat. And they were surprisingly good, as hungry as we were, despite the strong musk pike exude, and the picket-fence of large and small bones that northern offer. They were good that fist night; the second night they were not so good, and the last three days we choked them down, washed down with clear, cold lake water.

The weather lasted five days, but even on the sixth, the big lake was too rough, especially with an uncertain motor. And then a piece of good fortune, as a large inboard appeared, hugging the shoreline but in now danger from the wild waters.

I'll never be sure if it was the crazed and haggard look, or Anne's orange gloves (an afterthought, but perhaps our most valuable possession). At the first sound of the powerful engine, Anne had grabbed her gloves and, in a frenetic display of energy, had crashed through the brush to the Saganaga side of the island,

and the big boat had immediately come to our rescue. They tied our frail craft to the rear, and plied us with hot coffee for the last ignominious leg of our trip.

I was simply embarrassed, but Anne seemed immediately at home on the luxury craft, and even joined the crew in poking fun at our bedraggled equipment—very poor taste, I thought— and the trip home was ominously silent. Nonetheless, our marriage survived. Anne is both resilient and forgiving, fortunately, and even willing to travel with me into some other inhospitable situations through our long marriage. We have never intentionally fished for northern pike again, however, and I've tried to set limits on our adventures together.

Reader: There's that, and I also think you were just very lucky in marrying someone who will put up with you.

PPR: I suppose there is that possibility. Shall we go fishing? You call your wife, I'll call mine.

A SIDEBAR ON
PISCATOR'S WIFE

WHEN ANNE AND I BEGAN KEEPING company, it was 1957. We were both just out of (different) colleges, I an English major and Anne a physical therapist. The draft was breathing down my neck, I was unemployed, and it was the worst of times to meet the best of women.

Our "dates" were cheap: the zoo, small restaurants, movies, and eventually fishing. A friend told me of a backwater on the St. Croix River which was crawling with really big northern, and I invited Anne to come along, both for company and to impress her with my skills as a provider. The first night we scrambled down a precipitous bluff to a sandy beach overlooking a backwater pond that could not have been more than four feet deep anywhere. Not very promising, I said, playing my old experienced fisherman role—and then we started hooking eight- and ten-pound pike. I had brought a rod for Anne, thinking again that she could fumble around until she needed my manly advice.

When we left a few hours later, I helped her carry a fourteen- and a sixteen-pound fish back up that bloody bank. We drove to my parents' house, took pictures, cleaned the fish—and I didn't see her again for a week. A really dumb move for someone already crazy about a new girlfriend, but I was twentyish and not sure whether women or fish were more important.

At the end of the week, in early evening, I called her and met at her place—with an eighteen-and-one-half-pound monster I'd just pulled from those propitious waters. They'd not only shown me what Anne was like, but let me preserve my dignity and imagined superiority as a fisherperson.

So it all worked out, even though I was too dumb at the time to realize what a catch I had made. It was not so much that Anne loved to fish—and camp, and hike, and travel, and spend lots of outdoor time—but that she understood what fishing was like, and what life with a fisherman would be like, and accepted it. As excellent a quality in a woman as a voice that's soft and low.

Since, for almost fifty years, Anne has gone a-fishing with me everywhere. Not that she is a "serious" fisherperson all the time: If the fish are biting, whether it's big pike or a swarm of eager sunnies, she'll go at it with a will, and kill. But if the action slows, or if the fishing involves a fly rod and clambering over slippery rocks in icy water, she would rather look for agates or settle in with a good book.

Her best qualities as a fisherman's wife are her patience and her tolerance, and of course her skill in the camp kitchen. These are essential to anyone who's going to wander off for hours or days, with or without her, and return dirty, wet, muddy, sometimes smelling of strong drink, and often waving some miniscule trophy at her while grinning like an idiot.

She also must be willing to share a musty tent, travel some godforsaken back roads, tolerate temper tantrums when the four-wheel will not go any further or the only fly rod on board has somehow gotten snipped off in the door. And most of all, she must wait.

Now there is a real art to this virtue, and Anne has cultivated it to perfection. A good fisherman's wife must not love you too much; that is, if you're two hours late off the lake or stream she must be willing to accept that, yes, it's possible you drowned or had a heart attack, and that, if so, that's probably the way you'd like to go anyway. I've always pictured the ideal end a massive coronary from battling a huge brown in rushing water, and then the slow drift, me and the fish hooked together for eternity, down the river and away into that big sea at the end.

I digress. She must also love you enough so she doesn't want this to happen, and will begin to worry a bit if you're really late. But if it's a matter of just a few minutes, or an hour, she must recognize that that's normal for fishermen. There's always that last cast, or a sudden hatch of insects just at dusk, with big trout suddenly rising at one's feet. So Anne has developed a timetable: At dusk, she adds another half-hour for me to stumble off the stream to the car, another half-hour to bang and bumble my way off the back road and toward camp, another half-hour to clean fish, get tips from another fisherperson, untangle tackle, etc. Then she will just begin to allow herself to worry.

She says this is her plan, but I know she isn't always that philosophic, so I try to keep something close to a schedule. Also, as I go into my seventies and that final float down the big river becomes more likely, I carry a walkie-talkie, and will "check in" if my schedule has changed. That's an oxymoron, I'm afraid, as a "fisherman's schedule" is much closer to Indian time than Greenwich.

For those long periods in camp or motel or home when she's decided not to join me, Anne has her own interests: she's a rock-hound, reader, and cross-word enthusiast, and can entertain herself quite well alone, thank you.

Besides all these virtues, Anne is the perfect traveling companion, whether it's to a cozy tent at the end of a long trail, or to a cabin miles from any other human beings, or a crowded hotel at some famous mecca for trouters. We've spent a month in a VW bus on the road to Alaska, a summer traveling the West in a tiny Scamp-type trailer (twelve feet long!), and countless hours just pounding down the road to pursue some rumor of great fishing just over the mountain. We talk enough, but can also just enjoy the silence as we travel, and we can live in places without TV or radio: cribbage and books are the only real essentials.

I could never have found a better partner, even if I'd known what I was doing or how I'd spend the rest of my life. That includes all the rest of it, of course, beyond fishing, but I certainly wouldn't have been able to pursue that pleasure as extensively or happily as I have without the perfect fishing partner.

In return, I've taken her to places she will always remember, or we'll remember together, as sharing the sight of a sparkling river in the pines or a star-studded mountain night is half the pleasure. After I turned my attention almost entirely to trout, Anne learned that one of their great attractions was that trout have the nicest homes: where they live, in the cold clear streams of the West, is some of the most gorgeous country in the world, and we've spent weeks and months in it. The fishing sometimes is just a bonus. Being there with Anne has been the real joy.

TROUT MADNESS:
PART ONE

Piscator 1: "The Trout is a fish highly valued both in this and forraign Nations: he may be justly said . . . to be a generous Fish . . . a fish that feeds clean and purely, in the swiftest streams, and on the hardest gravel!" Izaak Walton, *The Compleat Angler*.

Reader: So now I know what not to do on a fishing trip. Your advice is contrary, sir, and thus far you've told me little of what things I should do, or where to go for good fishing. And I'm still hoping for a trout to appear before the book ends.

PPR: Gentle reader, be not impatient on either score, for first I have taught you as the best morality tales tell, by showing the evils to avoid on the road to good. My lesson, which you would have found appended to chapter last, had you read to the end, is that one must plan one's trip carefully, and gather all the necessaries for one's comfort, so that only fishing occupies your mind when you approach the water. As Norman MacLean says, "One great thing about fly fishing is that after a while nothing exists in the world but thoughts about fly fishing." The best of fishermen have empty minds, ridding themselves of all daily cares, and watching not the clock, but bringing eyes and hands and every thought to bear upon the moment, and the best approach to catch a wary fish. In other words, they must think like a fish.

Reader: Sounds pretty Zen to me. I do know what you mean, though: once I'm fishing, everything else seems to fade into the background, and I very often lose track of time entirely. And you say this is a good thing? My wife seems to think otherwise, and has even suggested that the next time I'm four hours late for supper she won't be there.

PPR: What happens while angling should have little to do with domestic cares, and even the greater passions can be laid to rest, at least for a time, while following the river. In one of Hemingway's stories, the hero can even briefly rest from the aftershock of war by thinking only of the stream and the fish before him. And if "The Big Two-Hearted River" can do that for the trauma of battle, think what it does for the lesser cares of everyday life. Thus you may call it Zen, or as one of our presidents did, a way to "cleanse your soul," but whatever it is, it makes the rest of life more bearable, and indeed joyous, knowing there are those splendid moments just around the next bend in the river.

Reader: But what about my wife? She says I already think like a fish, and also smell like a fish, and thinks I ought to take up golf instead.

PPR: Dear **Reader**, life is full of choices. One can waste hours chasing a piece of plastic and rubber over manicured grass, breathing fumes from golf carts and cursing each mistake, or any of a dozen other pastimes, but none will bring the peace and pleasures of the gentle art. There may be a price to pay, but that is between you and your wife . . . and your own inclinations. For me the choice was made long ago, and especially when I discovered the joys of trout.

Reader: Aha! Trout at last! Now you're going to tell me how to catch the one fish that has eluded me over the years and change my life.

PPR: Pursuing the king of fishes will bring change, I assure you, but it will mean even more time learning the arts of the angle, and perhaps traveling far from home to reach the pristine rivers where trout thrive. Are you willing to follow that far? And what about your wife?

Reader: You know, professor, there's another writer who says "women will forgive anything, or the species would have died out long ago." Think he's right?

PPR: He wasn't writing about fishing, you know, and that was science fiction.

Reader: Well, I don't see that there's much difference, except fishing stories tend to be more fantastic. Anyway, I hope he's right and that forgiveness does extend to fishing, because I'm ready to continue our journey in the quest for the elusive trout. I've tried it a few times, but that's been with spin rods, and what I really want is to catch them the classic way, on a fly rod. The problem is it's so hard to start. Everybody, it seems, read Norman MacLean or saw the movie of *A River Runs through It*, and decided that that would be the "in" sport for their generation. Not only was the scenery spectacular, and the fish large and plentiful, but the actual fishing was so beautiful. Now I'm afraid, to begin with, there will be too many of us out there.

PPR: There are always too many out there, if there's more than one. However, few will actually spend much time at trout fishing, in the end. They will find that the scenery is magnificent—trout live in the nicest homes—but that sometimes it takes a long walk and encounters with large animals and small insects to get there, and walking slippery-bottomed streams is not as simple as Brad Pitt made it look, nor is riding the current after a huge fish something most people want to try. The fish are still there, although not in the numbers of MacLean's youth, nor are they as easily fooled as in the movies. A few days of slogging through the brush in waders and catching few fish will send many away. To those who want only to look good, to fish with that panache that MacLean's hero displays, they'll find it takes more than a quick lesson with one of the fly-casting schools that have sprung up everywhere, and to fish with style and place a fly correctly are beyond some more. Then to learn what lures to use when, how to read the currents and the weather and the mood of the fish—those are the things that will send many neophytes home, or back to the spinning rod. It's really too bad—some of them might become good flyfishers, given some time—but it's not a sport for the impatient, or the competitor, or the meat-hunter. On the other hand, if they did succeed, the streams would be even more crowded, and in the end it should be only those willing to take the time and respecting the fish and the streams who should continue the quest. I have recently fished Montana again, and although there are more fishermen, I had no trouble finding streams with no other fisherman in sight, or places even on the blue-ribbon streams which were fished only once or twice a day.

PART TWO:
THE TROUT AND I: A
FISHY AUTOBIOGRAPHY

In 1966 THREE THINGS HAPPENED that changed my life. I was thirty-one years old, an instructor with no chance of promotion until I finished a doctorate. In March of that year my first son, Owen, was born, and so I got serious about my life and career. Paradoxically, early that year a new colleague, Tim Hansen, arrived fresh from Oregon with stories of trout and salmon fishing on the river-rich coast—and with fly-tying skills that he offered to teach me, starting me on a life-long quest.

Now I had already done some trout-fishing, and had used a fly rod a bit, but as often I would fish with spinning rod and either spoons or bait. I had admired those who were skilled with the fly rod, though, and felt instinctively that that was the "right way" to fish for trout. Once I began tying flies, it became the only way, and I vowed to improve my fly-rod skills along with learning to craft the flies themselves.

Tim started me on a fly that used almost everything one would ever need, at least in tying dry flies, and fortunately it was also one of the most successful fish-getters there is. The Rio Grande King uses a bit of tail-tinsel, yellow tail feathers, a chenille body, white wings, and a double-hackle wrap of ginger and grizzly. Getting all that to work covered most of the basics, and I then went to the books for other patterns to try.

One of those I should mention, because despite its quirkiness it was very helpful. That is George Leonard Herter's *Fly Tying and Spinning Lure Making Manual*. Some readers may remember the wonderful, zany Herter's catalog, when their store in Waseca, Minnesota, offered everything from fly materials to canoes to bows and arrows, many of them carrying the Herter's brand name and all of them guaranteed to be the best in the world by George Leonard Herter himself. The catalogs, and the books, were written in terrible purple prose, and included not only George's and sons' experience with many of the products, but his opinion on everything under the sun. An ad for minnow buckets begins, "The Herter buckets are tough and durable. You cannot put your fingernail into them and tear a piece of the foam plastic out like you can on foam plastic buckets . . . We will not make the fragile lightweight foam buckets made by some competitive makers as they are worthless and will not stand up." And in his books you will find only the Right Way (the Herter way) to do everything: from shooting a bow to tying a fly to making a peanut butter sandwich! Even domestic life is covered in one pamphlet titled "How to Live with a Bitch." The catalogs were always interesting, if sometimes laughable or infuriating, but the advice on fly tying was typically direct, very detailed, and with good illustrations of dozens of fly patterns. It was a good "starter book" for someone with no idea of what a bodkin was, or the difference between a Hendrickson and an elk-hair caddis.

With that and Tim's advice, I started to learn something of the variety of patterns available, and what they imitated. In fact, tying flies is not a bad way to begin one's trout fishing experience. Even before hitting the water, the fly tier will have some idea of what to use in what conditions of water and hatch, and what is produced in the long winter months at the vise can pay off in better fishing come spring. It's certainly not essential that a trout fisherman also is a fly tier, but there is an extra bit of satisfaction in having the fish hit something one has created. There's also the very practical advantage of being able to "match the hatch" almost immediately, if the fisherman has a fly-tying kit along on his/her fishing trips.

Now what all this also means, I found very quickly, was a need for all kinds of material not available in most local sporting goods stores. At the time I began, the only place to get tying materials was—yes, Herter's store in Waseca. The quality of their fly materials was, frankly, a little uneven, but they had a good selection of the basics. Also the quantities of furs and feathers was generous: I still have some packets with the Herter's label on them, some quarter century after the store went out of business!

Even when Herter's was peddling his wares, I discovered fly patterns that called for things he didn't carry, and before long I was looking to other sources—Dan Bailey's in Livingston, Montana, among others—for things like light bull elk hair, and kip tails, and an assortment of other esoteric pieces of animals that I'd never imagined existed. There was no Internet then, of course, so my searches were limited to catalogs and word of mouth, but I already thought it would be nice to visit some of these other stores to check out materials more directly.

There was also the "real world" source for materials. I have always hunted, but now I was more selective than in the past: a wood duck, for instance, became not only table fare but a source for some of the most-valued feathers in fly-tying, and a pheasant a treasure-house of assorted colored quills. I admit to casting a covetous eye on certain road-kill as well, although I generally ended up passing them by. Farm animals were another story, and living in the country I easily found sources for a few duck pointers here, some turkey feathers there. Another fly-tier and I even bought a gorgeous rooster, a Plymouth Rock I believe, who was a walking treasure-house of grizzly hackle.

Of course herein lies the trap: One never has everything available for every fly, and I'd often be stuck with a half-finished "bug" in my vise, waiting for a piece of fur or feather to arrive in the mail. My "study" grew cluttered with packets and boxes of tinsel, floss, yarn, pointers, hooks, hackle and an amazing variety of tools: vises and hackle pliers, bodkins of various sizes and shapes, thread holders, head cement bottles, small scissors and scalpels and other precision instruments for making tiny creatures. Tying flies can become almost as obsessive as trout fishing itself, almost another activity for its own sake. I have met people who are passionate fly-tiers, and almost never fish, but find their pleasure just in the isolated creation of beautiful flies. It is, to some, a real art form.

I never reached that point, although I can imagine myself as an older man, unable to reach the streams anymore or wield a rod, taking vicarious delight in making the beautiful bugs. At that time, though, I was more interested in their application, and I spent more time searching out trout waters in Minnesota.

Therein lies a problem. Although Minnesota is a fishing delight, it has relatively few cold-water streams to support trout. There are the Lake Superior tributaries in the northeast, but they are generally very small and very difficult to access and fish. In the southeast, however, the unique "driftless area" that was untouched by the glaciers in their advance through the region, I found several river systems that were both accessible and also well stocked with both rainbow and brown trout. I explored the Root River and Whitewater in its various branches, and began using a fly rod for all my trout-fishing. I had no formal training, certainly not the rigorous Presbyterian training that Norman MacLean went through, but eventually I began to feel comfortable with fly-casting. I also began to learn more about which fly to use when, and what sizes worked best in what conditions, and all the minutiae that eventually make a successful trout-fisherman.

Now for some of the long-promised advice, although it may or may not be helpful. It's at this point, or long before, that many would-be fly fishermen give it all up. They may have gone so far as to buy a nice matching rod, reel, and line, after learning all the variations of floating/sinking, level and double-taper, and various weights of lines to match particular rods, and they may even have taken a class that has brought them to a fairly high level of skill quickly, and then they go off to purchase a fly, as a kind of after-thought. In the catalog or sports store, they are confronted by row on row of colorful bugs—nymphs, streamers, wet and dry, big Muddler Minnows down to #28 midges, and in patterns and colors of bewildering variety. One of the many good fly books available, simply titled *Flies*, by J. Edson Leonard, lists over 2,200 varieties! And Leonard's book is from the 1960s, before the introduction of many variations and innovations, like the "spare" patterns and parachutes and whole new systems that have created hundreds more possibilities. It can truly be overwhelming to the beginner. The best advice I can give is to ignore it, at least at the start.

My fly-tying teacher passed on a bit of wisdom I've found helpful. An older trout fisherman, who taught him the Rio Grande King, said that if they won't hit that basic black fly, they probably aren't hitting, and you probably should quit. Now no true trouter actually does that, but it is true that, if the fish are feeding well, a few basic flies should get hits. After that, if you want to keep trying, you'll get into some of those 2,200 varieties, but a few at a time and only those that seem to match the hatch of the moment.

For someone just starting, a half-dozen flies in a range of colors and sizes should be successful about eighty percent of the time—if the fish are hitting at all. Try these for starters. Something in "basic black," a Rio Grande King or Black Gnat, a few gray or gray-blue, like the Adams or Hendrickson or Blue Wing Olive. Add several brown/tan flies, including Elk Hair Caddis and Light Cahill, a colorful all-purpose Royal Coachman or Royal Wulff or Trude (really all the same pattern), and another light-colored, flashy fly like the Gray Hackle Yellow or one of the sparkle patterns of Light Morning Duns. Get each in at least two sizes. Generally speaking, small flies (18 to 20 or even smaller) are more effective especially in clear or relatively still water. And if all these are still too confusing, just pick out a range of dry flies in basic colors, then start learning the names. (Label your fly boxes. I still can't memorize all the flies I use.)

Add to these dry flies a few nymphs when they just are not rising. Here the most basic are Pheasant Tail, Prince, and Hare's Ear patterns, and I've had good luck with the bead-head variety, in part because they sink more quickly, but probably because the flash of gold is attention-getting. I'm not especially fond of nymph-fishing, but neither am I a purist, and if there are no rise-forms on the water, chances are the nymph is a better bet.

If there's no visible hatch, but a few fish are rising, start out with the black or gray patterns. I admit I use the Rio Grande King or Black Gnat about fifty percent of the time, when there's no real indicator of what the fish are taking. If the water is swarming with brown or tan flies, obviously you begin with a Caddis or Light Cahill—and it'll probably work, but not always. Trout are tricky, and they may not actually be feeding on the insect filling the air at the moment: those rises may be to something else, some small creature just emerging but not even visible yet. Every fisherman has had the humbling experience of standing in the middle of a swarm of insects, with fish rising everywhere around him, and trying fly after fly which the trout completely ignore.

Nobody said it would be easy, but this may give the beginner a starting point from which to learn more about the infinite variety of patterns, while actually fishing with a fly. It'll also encourage the inevitable study of the kinds of insects trout generally feed on, which is a whole other subject. You needn't become an entomologist, but at some point you'll want to know what those little fur-and-feather things are imitating, and learn to recognize them when they're covering the water or filling the air. And best of all, with these few flies you'll almost certainly start catching a trout or two, and even a small trout on a light fly rod in fast water will get your heart pumping, and probably keep you out there until it's too dark to tie on another fly. And then you'd better stumble to the bank, because you're already half an hour late and an hour from home.

More on Trout:
Learning the Water

Reader: Okay, now you've actually given some advice. Whether it works or not I'll see. However, you said pages ago that three things happened to change your life, and you've only mentioned two: your son being born and learning to tie flies. There must be more to getting hooked (pardon me) on trout fishing, and I assume it's the third thing.

PPR: Sir, I appreciate your attention, and you're right. In 1966, because of my son's birth and the certainty that I didn't want to be an instructor all my life, I decided to pick up more classes leading to a Ph.D. In the hustle of everyday life, though, I waited until almost summer before registering anywhere, and then found few schools were still taking students for summer classes. After lots of frantic long-distance calling, I found only two admissions offices that would still take me in, one was in Iowa, and the other the University of Montana in Missoula.

Mankato, Minnesota, is a lovely place, in the center of the richest farmland on earth, hence the Blue Earth County encompasses it. It's generally flat, with miles and miles of soybeans and corn—not unattractive in its way, but monotonous. Since it was time for some real change, and since I'd been in the West before and liked it, I decided not to go to Iowa where there'd be more corn and soybeans, but go study where there would also be moutains and pine trees and dry air and, yes, probably a river or two to fish. Hence I packed up a few things, including my still-new fly rod and a box of home-tied flies and left for Missoula, Montana, in my VW Karmann Ghia.

I was there five weeks, and I fell in love. The university was okay. I studied Milton and Spenser, and worked hard mornings and late evenings at my classes, but then I had the afternoons free. I liked Missoula a lot. In the mid-sixties, the town was still fairly conservative, but there were coffee shops opening downtown and the smell of hemp was in the air. It was and is a strange mix: this is still Republican country, and even the home of some ultra-right militant groups, along with neighboring Idaho, but around the university the sixties came and stayed. Students wander from coffee shop to bookstore to army surplus store in standard hippy attire, and the writers' workshop attraced "outsiders" with a whole range of political views. It was no longer Norman MacLean's insular small town, but neither was it wholly modern: on the same streets with the ad agencies and fancy gift shops were men in boots and worn western hats, parking their F350 pickups complete with gun racks, and occasionally wearing a side-arm. And among them were the students or hangers-on who form another, far more liberal community. It was a strange and wonderful mix, and for the most part this diversity worked, and I enjoyed the town from the beginning, and still do, even though it's grown tremendously and now has malls and espresso kiosks extending as far as the eye can see, down toward the Bitterroot Valley and all along the Clark's Fork, which runs through town.

And those are what I really fell in love with: the rivers, big and little, that flow through and around and nearby, the Jocko and Lolo and Bitterroot and Clark's Fork, the Big Blackfoot of MacLean fame, and Rock Creek and a half-dozen others within driving distance of Missoula. I started tentatively, exploring the Clark's Fork itself where there was access near the city, and then began ranging out in the VW. The Ghia was not an ideal vehicle for the back roads, but I managed to get into some of the best trout water in the country without getting stuck or breaking down. Right from the beginning, in the Clark's Fork, I caught fish up to eighteen or nineteen inches, and found that fishing the big rivers was an entirely different game. Wading was more difficult, of course, and more dangerous; but almost all the rivers in the area were wadeable. It was more a matter of techniques. Some of the flies I'd used on the little Whitewater in Minnesota still were effective, especially my old reliable Rio Grande King. However, some flies I'd only read about really worked well too, the bigger flies like the Muddler Minnow and Wulff patterns. I had a wild day on the Big Blackfoot using #10 and 12 size flies, when every other cast brought a hit of some kind.

That is, once I found the spot the fish were feeding. As is often the case, it was along the edge of a long run, just where it met the still, deep water below, but on the Blackfoot, this crease was a long ways out. By wading almost chest deep, I could just reach it with my best casts. So I started improving my casting as well, and learned how to throw a longer line. Overall, I'm not an advocate of "far and fine." The "fine," as light a leader as possible, is always a good idea, but most of my fish over the years have been within easy casting range, even in relatively clear water. If one is moving upstream, and doesn't mess up with bad casts, the fish will generally let one get within easy range. However, in this and some other cases, there's no choice: one must be able to get the fly out some distance, and from an awkward position in the water. Although I prefer a short, light rod, I found that on the Clark's Fork and the Blackfoot the longer rod gave me a definite advantage for distance.

I'd been hanging around the rivers and fly shops long enough by this time to have heard of Rock Creek, the fabled stream just east of Missoula at Clinton, and finally made the trip down I-90 to Rock Creek Road. If I had fallen in love with the area, here was the spot that I would return to with a real passion for years to come. Rock Creek is a perfect trout stream—or river, really. It's quite wadeable, but also very deep in places. It also has a slick bottom, on smooth rock, and can be treacherous. That slickness is part of the richness of the river, of course. There are lots of nutrient in the water, although it's crystal-clear, hence lots of insect life as well. Hence lots of trout, of several varieties. In the upper half of its forty-mile run, there more cutthroat and cutthroat-rainbow cross, as well as bull trout, while rainbow and some big browns predominate in the lower stretches.

That first trip I didn't get far beyond the first bridge on Rock Creek Road. I'd worked my way that far, catching fish occasionally. It was a warm, sunny afternoon in July, not the best time for trout, but as always there were a few fish rising, and my Rio Grande Kings enticed several into hitting. At the bridge there's a run into a deep pool, a much-used "hole," with easy access, but on this day I had it to myself. I caught two trout on dry flies, and then the action stopped. As I've said, I'm not a purist: I tied on a Lady Mite nymph, something new to me but which seemed effective. On my first long cast, the fly was in the deep water at the end of the run, and I gave it one last twitch before bringing it back—and it stopped dead. I assumed I was hung up, but of course then it exploded, and I was into my first twenty-inch fish. It stayed in the pool, but I couldn't bring it in. I remember someone pulling up as I played the fish, and asking why I didn't land it, and I said it was going to do what it wanted. I didn't have much choice, nor did I really want a conversation just then. I had my hands full for fifteen or twenty minutes, but finally brought in a great fat brown, yellow-gold and glittering trout.

Obviously, I would spend many more days on Rock Creek during that first trip, and over the years I would return to explore all of it. I had just begun, on the Blackfoot and now on Rock Creek, to learn the likely places fish would feed, and how different every piece of water was on every river. That, and learning what the fish wanted—from a hatch swarming around my face, to an apparently lifeless, riseless sheen of river—would occupy a large part of the rest of my life. I was just starting to learn to think like fish.

TO TIE OR NOT TO TIE:
IS IT A QUESTION?
(ANOTHER DIGRESSION)

FOR MANY OF US WHO HAVE ALWAYS TIED, it may seem academic: of course you tie, as well as fish. And there are lots of reasons to make up your own lures, but also some very good ones for simply buying flies as you need them. Some of it has to do with age, some with cost, and most with inclination. That is, do you want to spend the time at your tying vise, or would you rather spend it fishing?

I actually started tying flies before I had done much trout fishing. Tim Hansen, from Oregon, got me really interested in the delicate, beautiful little insects that he crafted on his time off from teaching (and fishing), and gave me my first lessons in putting together a trout fly—dry flies only, as that was Tim's specialty both tying and fishing. Actually, I have also spent most of my time with dry flies. It's not that I never fish anything else, but tying nymphs is, by comparison, rather boring. Perhaps as a result, I've never become a very good nymph fisherman, nor do I enjoy it nearly as much as surface flies. I've tried a few of the "in-between," all-purpose flies like the Muddler Minnow, and they're both interesting to tie and fish, but for something that gives real satisfaction just in the making, I prefer the dry fly to all others.

Therein lies the trap. In talking with an old acquaintance recently at a class reunion, I discovered that he too had begun trout fishing—at age sixty-five—and was enjoying it tremendously. He was retired, and had begun traveling all over the world seeking out good new trout waters. When he learned that I also tied most of my flies, he wondered whether he should begin doing that, to improve both his knowledge of insect life and his chances of matching the hatch. I hesitated, but then said I didn't think he should start: buy what flies you need and enjoy the fishing.

At the time I didn't explain my reasoning, but it's something like this: if you start tying early on, it becomes an integral part of your fishing over the years and doesn't really interfere with the time spent on the water. For someone sixty-five years old and just beginning, it would become a tremendous commitment of time and resources that could be spent fishing. That's part of the trap. The other is one I mentioned earlier: just making flies, varying the patterns, trying new forms can be so fascinating in itself that it becomes its own end. Now if you have become infirm, or quite elderly, there's nothing wrong with this creative pleasure, but if the thrill of making flies is in fooling real live trout with them, it can become an interference, a vicarious substitute for the real thing. If you love fishing and all its attendant pleasures, nothing should lure (excuse me) you from the watery world of the trout. It's also not a question of ability: if you can still fish at sixty-five or seventy, you probably also can still tie flies. The acquaintance I mentioned was an eye surgeon, and probably had far better technical skills and coordination than I have.

There's also the matter of equipment and materials—not just the expense, because they will more than pay back their cost over a few years—but the time spent getting "all the right stuff" for tying numerous patterns. It's always annoying to the beginner to start tying a pattern and realize he/she is missing some basic ingredient—some grizzly hackle just the right size, or some light elk hair for a caddis, or turkey wings for some Muddler Minnows. There is, to begin with, quite a list of equipment that's absolutely necessary and some that's just very useful. The list of materials you'll eventually want to have on hand is practically limitless, as you tie more and more patterns in smaller and larger sizes, and it's surprising how much time it takes to: first, find out what you need, and, second, to gather everything from stores or catalogs. And if that's time you would more happily spend fishing, it's probably not worth it.

If you are just beginning to fish trout, however, tying your own flies has some real benefits. The first is simply practical: a good dry fly now costs, on average, $1.50 to $2.50, depending on the type and the store. To be even modestly equipped, the fly fisherman needs fifteen or twenty dry flies and a half dozen nymphs. Most trouters carry many more, often fifty or sixty in those bulging vest pockets, and they probably have a hundred or so stocked in camp or home. That's a big investment to begin with, or to build up to, either way, and when you start fishing those little tree-infested creeks, or making the long back-cast into a steep, rocky streamside, you'll inevitably cast out a line with the fly no longer attached. If you're very lucky, you'll be able to retrieve a few of these: if it's just hung up. Okay, you follow the line back and climb the tree, or maybe even pull it loose. More often, it's out of reach and the leader snaps before the fly lets loose. Or if it's snapped loose on the backcast, you'll have no idea where to begin looking.

It is inevitable to lose flies. That's as much a part of the sport as occasionally taking a dunk in the river. Both are annoying, but wet pants don't cost you anything. Those lost flies, remember, are two dollars wasted, fed to the trees. If you tie your own, the materials will probably cost something less than two bits a fly, again depending on the pattern. They'll also have some sweat equity in them, but it's a pleasant labor, and shouldn't have a wage placed on it. So you're probably saving about eighty percent of the cost of "store-bought" flies if you tie your own, and even if it's still annoying to lose them, that takes some of the sting out of it.

There's also the advantage of learning more about the feeding habits of trout, and what they will take during a particular season or under various conditions. You needn't become a professional entomologist to catch trout, but you should at least recognize that if there's a hatch going on, and the fish are feeding on it. You ought to look closely at what color and size the bugs are that the trout wants to eat at that moment. Your fly may not exactly match that insect—few flies are really perfect imitations of anything live—but it should at least be the same basic color, and should definitely be about the same size. I've found that it's often more effective to change fly size, if you think you have the colors right, than to change patterns completely.

You can also make up flies as you need them, if you start carrying a portable kit. It may save you a long trip to the store if you don't have the particular pattern or size the fish seem to be taking, or if you've used up all the appropriate flies. This doesn't have to be elaborate—I carry along a large tackle box with most of the basic equipment and materials I'll need, and it's saved not only some time, travel, and money, but more important, salvaged many a fishing trip.

In winter, for most of us there is little or no actual fishing, but you can spend hours getting ready for the coming season. That's obviously the time to stock up, both on flies and on materials that have run short, or that are needed for a new fly. It not only helps pass the time until you can finally get out on the stream, but once the season starts, you'll be fully equipped and ready to go.

Perhaps the best argument for tying your own flies is the pleasure that comes from having a trout hit something you have created. You'll have that in mind every minute you spend crafting a Light Cahill or a Royal Coachman: where and when will I use this, in an early hatch on the nearby Whitewater, or in July on the Gallatin River in Montana? You'll remember earlier takes on that pattern, just where you were and how big (or small) the fish were, so you have the vicarious pleasure of fishing at the same time you're creating something for the next time. And seeing a trout rise to that little concoction of thread, feathers, fur—and hook—is gratifying, a tribute to your workmanship. It may seem a small thing, proving that you're smarter than a fish, but believe me anyone who has tried to attract a finicky brown with a fly of his own making knows how good it feels.

It finally boils down to your own priorities. My own preference is to tie my own flies. I believe it helps make the more "compleat angler" of any fisherman. However, it is a somewhat fussy and certainly time-consuming craft, and if you want to spend every available minute out on the stream, that's admirable, and putting in hours bent over a fly-tying vise is not for you. Whichever choice you make, in the end it comes down to how effectively you can present the right fly in the right spot at the right time, and then all you can do is hope. At that instant it is the trout who's going to make the decision, and when he finally rises and you feel that electric pulse in your rod, you probably won't be thinking about whose fly it is that did the job.

FISH, FISH, EVERYWHERE

Reader: So you left your wife and new baby and spent two months fishing in Montana.

PPR: I prefer to say that I gave up my summer to return to my studies, striving to make a better life for those left behind.

Reader: And they were still there when you got back from fishing.

PPR: My wife is a very tolerant woman, but also not gullible. I talked a great deal at first about Milton and Spenser, I thought with some enthusiasm: but there was the smell of woods and streams and trout about me, and she was well aware what had excited my passion while I was gone, especially when I couldn't help babbling about the huge fish I'd caught and the country I'd wandered through. She is tolerant, but she also made it clear that I wouldn't make the trip alone again.

Reader: So she went with you on all your future trips?

PPR: Not all, but a dozen times in the next thirty-five years. She is still not a flyfisher, but she loves the country where trout live as much as I, and is a better camper. Shortly after my first trip, we took a tent and spent idyllic weeks on Rock Creek. Missoula now became the place to visit, and it became onerous to have to go to town. We began to explore the rest of Montana, and Idaho, and Wyoming, and I realized that one lifetime was not enough to fish even all the rivers in Montana.

Reader: Maybe if I took my wife along, she'd begin to understand what I love about fishing, and also why I'm still late getting home for dinner.

PPR: Maybe. On the other hand, you must balance your life—your life and your wife—and not spend all your time fishing. I'm only supposed to advise you on fish, so I haven't talked much about other things, but in my own life there were lots of other things going on as well. After all, your career, your family, your home life are also important.

Reader: Oh, so now you're telling me not to fish so much, after hooking me on trout, Montana, and fly-tying. Thanks a lot.

PPR: You must find a way to reconcile all those things, believe me, or you'll lose either the pleasure of fishing, or your happy home.

Reader: So how did you manage this? You spend more time fishing than anyone I know, but you haven't talked about becoming a professor and keeping your wife happy. How did you manage that?

PPR: I went to Albuquerque.

Reader: What?

 THE BALANCED LIFE

PPR: In 1968 I moved, with my wife and two small sons, to New Mexico. I had only recently become addicted to trout fishing, and logically should have moved west. However, my career got in the way: I needed the Ph.D. to advance in rank, and the University of New Mexico offered one with a strong program in American literature, my area of specialization.

As it turned out, we loved Albuquerque and New Mexico, and I did find some good fishing in the Rio Grande itself, and eventually followed it north into Colorado, where it produces some really large trout.

There is also excellent fishing in the San Juan River and in a number of small streams in the north, around Eagle's Nest and the Red River area, but I found nothing to match the possibilities found in Montana, Wyoming, and Idaho.

Reader: So when you finished your Ph.D., you went to Montana.

PPR: No, we returned, in fact, to Minnesota, and we commuted to Montana. Remember, I too have a wife, and a life, and, as it happened, the best job available when I had finished my doctorate was—back in Mankato, at Minnesota State University. And that's where I spent the next twenty-five years, eventually becoming a full professor of English.

Reader: So you didn't "follow your bliss," and live a life of fly-tying and trout-fishing?

PPR: Yes and no. I did, in fact, follow my bliss; but that's another story. This is a story of fishing, and although I lived a full, happy professional and personal life, I spent a good portion of it pursuing the art of the angle. You see, that's the big thing you must learn: life is more than fishing, but without the fishing, it would be not nearly so rich or full.

Reader: Well, I'm disappointed. I bought your book, and I've spent time and money following your advice, and done everything possible to fish whenever and wherever I could. Now you say fishing is not that important.

PPR: Oh, I didn't say that. As the cliche goes, "Fishing is not a matter of life and death; it's more important than that." What one must do, however, is find the life that will allow as much fishing as possible and still live a productive life in the world.

 A FISHING MANIFESTO:

1. MARRIAGE AND WORK ARE ALMOST INEVITABLE, and even desirable. However, one must be very careful in both cases that they not interfere with fishing. Thus, the wife one chooses must be either an outdoor enthusiast or very tolerant, or preferably both, and the work one does, even if it requires much time and effort, must allow for flexibility and large amounts of free time.

2. IF POSSIBLE, FIND WORK THAT FIRST, allows one to live near or preferably on some fishable lake or stream. You'll want to range farther afield of course for variety, but one ought to have access to some acceptable, everyday place to fish. If that is not possible, you must either accept the fact that you'll spend more time driving than fishing. The better solution would be to find a new job, or a new place.

3. BUY ONLY THE FISHING EQUIPMENT that you absolutely need. If you fish lakes and rivers and oceans, bass, pike, walleye, trout, sailfish, and dorado, among others, you will need a great variety of rods, reels and lures, to say nothing of a boat and motor or two. In other words, you will need absolutely everything. This may at times conflict with Number 1 (above), and you must be careful not to spend more than you make—although it's always possible to do without frills like lawnmowers and new clothes. Or, better still, sell some old equipment that you no longer need and buy new things. (This makes it appear that you're really not getting more, just replacing what you have). Do not spend more than your wife needs: lawnmowers, yes; new kitchen equipment, no. That you must buy, and scrimp elsewhere. Included in essential equipment is a serviceable car or truck, to be used primarily for fishing trips. It is unsettling to some women to catch their hair in a fly dangling from a fly rod, or to drive any distance with a container of once-live bait. Also this vehicle will be perpetually filthy, inside and out, and it is easier to get another car for your wife than to try keeping it immaculate. That is not only wasted effort, but may lead you to other time-wasting habits, like cleaning mud off your boots or putting your catch in sealed containers before dumping them in the vehicle.

4. CULTIVATE LOCAL FISHERMEN, WHEREVER you go, learn what they can teach you, and then go your own way. Often their advice is valuable. Just as often it's limited by what they've always done, and you may do better trying something new. By all means don't intrude on their favorite spots, or interrupt them when they're fishing, and follow good fishing etiquette everywhere (that is, don't jump upstream of another stream fisherman, and don't even think of fishing near someone else, in boat or stream, without asking permission). And don't trespass to get to that nice stretch of water. It's not only rude, but in some places may get you shot!

5. GIVE YOUR OWN ADVICE FREELY, but only when asked for it, and tell exactly the truth. No one expects that, and no one will believe it. If you are trapped with a big stringer of bass, you must at least tell another fisherman where you hooked them, but you needn't be precisely accurate about the lure you've used, if you plan to fish there again. With trout, you should always tell what fly you're using. Chances are the arriving fisherman will have a different pattern or size, and anyway the trout will probably have changed feeding patterns by that time. In all cases, tell the truth, but you may wish to "tell it slanted." Become an oracle by giving your answers in riddles or metaphorically, and everyone will believe you actually have all the answers, because they can't understand them.

6. YOU MAY WANT TO TALK ABOUT "the big one that got away," but if you do it too often, others will begin to question both your veracity and your abilities. Of course, no one expects truth from fishermen anyway, but it's much more satisfactory to walk nonchalantly (and silently) into camp with a twenty-four-inch trout than to display your broken leader or empty creel.

7. WHETHER TO CATCH AND RELEASE or keep fish is a personal matter, to some degree. I still like an occasional trout dinner, and I'll spend an hour cleaning a mess of sunfish or filleting a couple of bass, but for the most part, I now release most of the fish I catch. On the other hand, those who catch more than their limit or take one limit home and come back to catch another should spend hell fishing a water-filled bomb crater, like one of Tim O'Brien's shell-shocked heroes.

8. DO NOT MAKE FISHING a competitive sport. Of course you want to bring in a good stringer of fish, or catch the biggest one, but making that the aim of your fishing destroys the point of it all. It should be just you trying to outwit the fish, and thinking only of fishing, clearing your mind of all the other junk that may be going on, including the everyday struggles with your fellow human beings. Look into the water, keep your eyes and mind focused there, and in the beauty of the places fish live, and forget about beating the other guy. You'll enjoy it more, and you'll probably fish better.

9. YOUR CAR MAY BE A MESS, and someday you'll have to clean up that tangle of tackle in your garage, but never leave a mark on the waters. Pick up not only your coffee cup and worm can,

but those stray bits of nylon line and definitely those cigarette butts. The lakes and rivers should be for everyone forever, and you know good fishermen by the marks they don't leave.

10. FISHING IS VERY LIKE WRITING. If you don't have to do it, you probably won't—and shouldn't. Don't feel guilty because you'd rather work, and don't feel guilty because you'd rather fish.

COMMUTING TO
ROCK CREEK

PPR: As I said, we returned to Minnesota, and it has been a wonderful place to live, work and fish. Nonetheless, the West continually beckoned, and I did try to get a professorship in Montana. However, those who live there went for the same reasons I wanted to go, and seemed never to leave, so appropriate positions were never available.

So I made the best of it, and traveled West whenever time and opportunity presented themselves. By this time Anne had heard so much of the beauties of Montana that she went with me most of the time, and fell in love with the mountains and rivers, if not the fish, as I had. Thus began another balancing act: living and working in Minnesota, and commuting to Rock Creek whenever possible.

PPR: My first return trips to Rock Creek, near Missoula, were in the 1960s, usually in the ubiquitous Volkswagen, and with a tent for a shelter. Jack Lawson, another professor from Mankato State University, and I made the trip a few times, and wife, Anne, and I have followed that trail west at least twenty times.

Geographic names are deceptive. Rock Creek is a river, bigger than the Maple or the Watonwan rivers here in Minnesota. It's crystal clear, with a rock bottom that's slippery as a waxed floor, and it's classed a Blue Ribbon stream, meaning it's full of trout. Starting near

Phillipsburg it runs almost fifty miles through the Sapphire Mountains down to the Clark's Fork near Clinton. Most of it is accessible from the gravel road that runs its entire length.

It's not wilderness, exactly. The upper reaches are small-ranch country, and the lower end now has lots of summer homes, one lodge and motel. But in between there are only forest service campgrounds and miles of fishable water. There are deer everywhere, a few moose, and the occasional bear, and a healthy flock of mountain sheep transplanted here years ago and thriving in the rugged slopes along the river.

My first half-dozen trips to Rock Creek were tent-stops in the Forest Service campgrounds, which are well maintained and offer water and outhouses (with metal seats that are torture on a cold mountain morning!). Jack and I were chased out once by a garbage-bear that wouldn't go away, but otherwise the campgrounds are idyllic spots, usually right on the river bank and often sheltering only a few other campers.

When showers became critical, we occasionally sneaked in to the Elkhorn Lodge, about ten miles up Rock Creek Road. Later, Anne and I began camping at the lodge regularly, and as we graduated from tent to trailers to RV, we used the Elkhorn as home. Besides showers, the lodge in recent years had a world-class restaurant, the Bluebird Café, and so there was nothing we needed from the outside world. In the evening deer wandered through the camp, and just up the road the sheep would start down the mountain for supper in the meadows beside the river.

In 2002, the Elkhorn and the café burned to the ground. The cabins remain, and it still operates as a cabin-rental resort only: no campers, and of course no restaurant. The last few years Anne and I have chosen to drive out in our Subaru wagon, and we rent a motel room at the Fisherman's Mercantile, just at the start of the Rock Creek Road. Neither of us wants to stay at the Elkhorn any more, because it breaks our hearts.

I'd never even thought of staying at the Merc when we camped at the Elkhorn and had never even looked at the rooms, but in 2003 I called Doug Perisco and rented a room for a week, sight unseen. We couldn't believe how luxurious they were! Not only were they huge, but bright and clean and fully furnished, some with complete kitchens. I know, I know: it's not camping, but it is fishing and it is comfortable, and, yes, we're getting older. We've earned our comfort, sleeping on pine boughs for mattresses and waking in sleeping bags with the temperature well below freezing. And we loved it all, but in our seventies the big warm rooms at the Merc are what our bodies and spirits need. And after all, if I'm going to fish all day. I need that comfort and a good night's sleep.

Rock Creek was one of my first experiences with western rivers, and it was love at first sight. That first summer in Missoula I had only a rudimentary knowledge of trout fishing, from a few forays on the small Midwest streams, and these creeks and rivers were new to me in every way. First, most of them are larger; you can wade Rock Creek and the Lolo and even the Blackfoot in some places, but you must be careful—they can drop off quickly, and you can't simply wade across, or even up, most of them. A fall can be not only cold and unpleasant but downright dangerous. Some, like the Big Horn, Yellowstone, and Madison are impractical for wading, although there are places on all where you can cast from shore. Float fishing is the best approach on these, and indeed is practiced on others like the Rock Creek and Gallatin, although I've always preferred wading.

Second, almost all have rock or heavy gravel bottoms, and that makes for tricky footing. On Rock Creek, the slipperiest of all, felt-bottomed boots are a necessity, or rather a minimum: spiked boots are better still, and even then your legs will feel the strain after a day's fishing: it's always a balancing act.

Third, there are miles and miles of water to fish, with every kind of flow and current the rivers can create. In its first stretch, just starting down into the Sapphire Mountains, Rock Creek consists of flat pastoral sweeps, with a few deep holes and a modest current. Partway down are the Dalles, a cliff region where chunks of rock the size of houses thrust up out of a wicked current, which spills and swirls rapidly around them. Below that are broad flats, the multicolored bottom like a palette under the sheet of glassy water, and then there are fast runs, with long pools below them and shores ranging from meadow to woods to shale beaches.

And, last, there are fish everywhere. You may catch them on those flat broad stretches that seem to shallow for anything to hide, but even on a sunny day they'll sometimes be rising there. In the Dalles, there will always be some trout hanging around the big rocks, waiting for a meal to drift by; and anywhere there's a fast run into a deep pool you know there will be trout.

To me it was a paradise, and if I had been only mildly interested in trout fishing before, Rock Creek seduced me. To be honest, that first summer I didn't catch a lot of fish. I had little idea of what flies to use, of how to read this more complex water system, and even of how to work a fly on the bigger waters. Yet I caught fish. I used the flies I'd started out with in Minnesota—the Rio Grande King and Grey Hackle Yellow and the Adams, as well as a few nondescript nymphs, and often enough I'd hook a fish or two. There were also times when there was an obvious hatch, and nothing I threw into the rising swarm of fish interested them in the least. (This still happens, to me and everyone, and is one of the fascinations and torments of fly fishing.)

But I caught fish. I caught rainbows that soared into the air at the first touch of the hook, and beautiful cut-throat and golden browns that drove to the bottom and taught me to sometimes just hang on for the ride until they were ready to come in. I was using a four-piece, nine-foot Garcia rod then, good for traveling but with little "backbone" and very little thrust when casting. It was limber, though, and if I was patient I could land most fish. So I caught fish, and they caught me, and Rock Creek captured me forever.

It is almost exactly forty years from my first trip here. I am sitting in the Rock Creek Mercantile half-listening to Doug Perisco, the owner, rant. Another "regular" is sitting to one side smoking an elegant pipe stuffed with Captain Black. I know, because I use the same to-bacco and in an emergency can borrow a pipeful. John is eighty-one, and looks about sixty. He's from the West Coast, and has been coming to Rock Creek about as long as I have.

Doug's rants are more formally available on his web page (www:/rcmerc.com). "Rant" is his own term. It's hard to tell whether it high good humor, the pleasure of holding forth, or high dudgeon sometimes. In the Merc his rants really carry more weight. He and his crew craft some of the finest flies available, and he really does know more about the river—from his own experience, or from gossip among fishermen—than almost anyone on the stream. At the moment, he's holding forth on one of his favorite topics.

The best fishing on Rock Creek is in March and April, but he can't seem to convince anyone of that and everyone comes to Montana in the summer, for some reason, and then is disappointed in the fishing. Which is not true, of course, as the fishing is nearly always good, and the summer in Montana is beautiful, but he's probably right about the fishing and someday I'll try coming in early spring. In the meantime, this is his way of welcoming us, who have just arrived in September as usual, for a one-week stay.

However, at the moment I'm more interested in looking at wading shoes with carbide studs in them. My legs ache from trying to balance my way this first day on the upper Creek, and at my age I'm trying to fish as comfortably as I can. John has recommended a fishing staff, but I've tried that before and it's just too much equipment. Half the time I'm dropping the staff to fish, then stumbling along because I'm too busy to pick it up again. John has also recommended not fishing as much, or casting from shore, which he now does, but I've never been able to do that either.

I decide on nothing. Doug insists on a strange-looking hopper for the evening fishing, a green sponge-like thing with those white bungee-cord legs. It's nothing like the beautiful Pale Morning Duns or Parachute Adams that I admire, and that he makes so well. In fact it's nothing like anything I've ever used, and very little like any grasshopper I've seen, but I buy a couple even though I think I know better, and will tell Doug so tomorrow. In the meantime I'll fish just a short ways from the Merc, where the wading is not so difficult.

And of course when I get to a favorite spot just above the bridge to Valley of the Moon Ranch my first cast with the green glob brings a swirl and bulge of a heavy fish, and in a few minutes I net a seventeen- or eighteen-inch brown. Then it doesn't work anymore, and the fish are rising ahead of me, around me, and nothing works, just as in my earliest days. I switch flies frantically. There's no obvious hatch, nothing in the air, but the fish are working just as hard as I am, sucking something from the surface. It has to be something small, so I go to #20 flies, and finally get a hit on a diminutive Light Cahill. For half an hour I hook nice fish, twelve to sixteen inches, on that fly or anything small and light or white-colored, and then it's over.

I admit to Doug that his green glob worked, but only once, then tell him about the small light flies, which he thinks over for a minute and then identifies what it probably was (he's familiar with the real insects in all their forms, which I am not), and by the time he's done it's obvious that he'll be pushing small Light Cahills for a few days, and that it will be his idea. That's all right. That's how you get to be the sage of Rock Creek.

I spend most of the next week fishing only up as far as the Dalles, and even that only a few times. I know the water from the Merc on up to the Elkhorn best anyway, and it has some of the best fishing. The Dalles is hard work, but it's spectacular, and I never can skip it entirely. I wade carefully along the big rocks and near the deep pools, and I'm back to standard flies in the daytime—Rio Grande Kings and Adams and Elk Hair Caddis. The fishing here is sometimes startling. A big cutthroat will come out of nowhere, in five feet of water or in a fast run along a rock, and often he'll be on before I even see him hit. Then it's a battle to get the fish out of the heavy current and try to guide him to someplace relatively shallow.

It's still hard work—I haven't popped for the carbide studs yet, although it's almost inevitable that I will. My other equipment has improved since my first days on Rock Creek, though. At least I use felt bottoms on my waders now, and have a couple of nice limber rods to choose from. Years ago I found a sweet little Fenwick, only seven feet long but with fine action and good backbone for a short rod. It was handy on the small streams in Minnesota, but I also found I enjoyed working it out West too. I've handled fish over twenty inches with this little stick, and the smaller ones feel like lunkers. It won't cast quite as far as a longer rod, but I'm not into long distance. Most of the fish I catch are within thirty or forty feet, and I can drop a fly pretty accurately at that range. That rod finally went the way of all rods—snapped in a car door—and I never could get an exact duplicate, but I do have another Fenwick, seven and one-half feet, and an assortment of others. One of my favorites is another seven-footer from Cabela's, which is just about as sensitive as my old Fenwick, and I do have rods up to nine feet, just in case I need to reach out and touch someone. That "just in case" is the fisherman's credo, and his downfall. One must have duplicates (and triplicates, and multiples) of everything for a particular situation (which seldom seems to arise twice), or for backup when a rod breaks. You certainly need several flies of every pattern and size, since there's nothing worse than finally finding the lure the fish want, and then losing it—and finding you have nothing exactly like it, or the wrong size.

Good lines are the second essential after rods, and I soon learned to get a good match for each stick in my arsenal. Although all good rods tell what weight is appropriate, you may find after a little use that you actually need the next smaller weight, or more usually, the next larger, to get a good whip in your rod. For years I used double tapers, simply because it was cheaper to be able to turn them around when one end wore out, but as I get older and time gets shorter, I've come to prefer weight-forward lines which just cast better. They may not last even a full season, if I'm fishing hard; but then I always have an extra in the tackle bag.

I'm amazed at what one can pay for a fly reel, which is really the simplest and least essential part of any fisherman's outfit. A reel doesn't really do much of anything—it just holds line, and you can use it to brake a fish's run—but essentially they're just for storage. Most fishermen I know play a fish with their left hand on the line anyway, and only start cranking when the fish is coming in. They don't "cast," like a spinning or bait-casting reel, have few moving parts, and are elementary in construction. That $300 reel will probably outlast something cheaper, but how long do you plan to live anyway? I still have reels I've used for thirty years, and if they're no longer precision instruments, they still function well enough for the simple job they do.

Now I'm ranting. Good equipment does help, and I would like a whole closet-full of Sage rods and matching

reels, but I'm not really convinced there's that much difference. I am sure I couldn't get a thousand dollars worth
more pleasure out of the top-of-the-line stuff, and I'd
feel uncomfortable with them in the woods. I'd also cry
a lot when I smashed one in the car door, and couldn't
afford to have several similar backups along.

So I'm trudging along below the Dalles, now, with my
perfectly adequate fishing gear and my felt-bottomed
waders. Further down, where the rapids end and the current is not so dangerous, fishing is more leisurely, although the rocks are still slick and there's plenty of deep
water. Still, there are places to wade across the river, and
runs that offer a hundred yards of easy fishing, casting
first just along the edge of the fast water, then further
into it with each cast. Even if there are no fish rising, I'll
often get a hit in these feeding lanes, and if there's a
hatch, and there are rise-rings here and there, and I have
some idea what to use, I can catch fish after fish.

I release almost all that I catch these days. On Rock
Creek you can only keep a couple between twelve and
sixteen inches, and today I'll take those two for supper—usually closer to twelve, as I have come to believe
the smaller "pan-size" fish actually taste better. I believe
in catch and release—mostly—but I'm certainly not a
purist, and I love a trout supper now and then. This is
a fish that is meant to be eaten—no scales, just gut and
throw in the pan—the perfect food, a little like the
"Shmoo" in L'il Abner (anybody else remember that?)
And there's more and more evidence that eating fish is
good for you, and eating the best fish must be even better nutrition. And besides, they taste wonderful.

I have a little problem with quitting fishing: there's
always "one more cast," and this is especially true in the

evening, when a hatch may start just at dark or even after, so I'm often fishing until I can't see the fly on the water, or can no longer get the leader into the eye. For that reason we often eat late. I gut my two fish, and stumble back to the car in the dark, then back to the motel. It's pitch dark now, of course, but Anne is not worried. She adds a half hour to sunset, then a half hour more for extra distance to the car, or from the car to home. After that she may begin to worry, but not seriously for another half hour. Fishermen are notoriously unreliable. I start up the little gas grill we've brought along, even before shedding my waders, spray on a little Pam, and get rid of my gear and wash up while the little fish sizzle. Anne has a salad and beans ready to go, and we have the feast of kings by the porch light on the bank of Rock Creek. Like my equipment, life on Rock Creek may not be absolutely perfect, but it's awfully damn close.

 # THE PLACES
FISH LIVE I

Reader: So Rock Creek is heaven, but I'm here in Minnesota, 1,200 miles away. I can get there once every couple of years, if I'm lucky. What do I do in the meantime?

PPR: Anyplace fish live will be beautiful, if in different ways, and Minnesota is also a grand place to start. Where you seek fish, you must first get to the water. It may be that muddy pond a few miles from home, or the sweet clear stream rippling over rock, the massive ebb and flow of the sea, or the thunder of great rivers. They all call to your blood, are mixed in to the very chemicals of your spirit that you go to them by instinct, seeking home.

And there are the fish, at home already. You look for them as you look at your own history, and they too call you, like the water with no consciousness of their beckoning.

Before you moved to the land, became hunter-gatherer, you were one with them, and now to seek them is to rejoin them, and even the eating is a reunion with what you were.

Now you travel a mile or five thousand in that journey. It is not the reasoning part of you that sends you out across the land, but something you may not understand at all, and call adventure or "vacation," when it is really not a leaving but a returning. The call that brings you to the water is deeper even than the drive that pushes salmon up the stream, more profound and often far less conscious than sex.

And so you walk, drive, fly to places water touches land, and linger on the shore or float on the surface, and come close, oh so close again, to home. You and I, we have come so far, and now we travel to return. And having chosen these elements, this way to live, far beyond our memory of choosing, we walk and drive and fly over the land. Where the water touches the land is nearly always beautiful, and the travel and the things we do along the way become another reason for this seeking.

FISH HAVE
BEAUTIFUL HOMES I

Most of the places you find good fishing you also find
yourself in beautiful country. Even that little muddy river will
have furnished the earth along its way with water to grow trees
and grass, and maybe it still supports a few fish. If you want better fishing, then you must find places that have been less used
by mankind, and that means you will find yourself in wilder and
more rugged landscapes. The journey to fish, then, is also most
often a journey into beauty, into scenery that can make the trip
worthwhile in itself.

From our home in Minnesota, there are two places that
stand out for fishing, and for the setting. I've fished for northern
pike, walleye, and bass countless times in the Boundary Waters
lakes, and even though the area is becoming more heavily used, it's
still big enough to withstand the traffic and still remain beautiful.
Regulation of the BWCA has become more strict, and that too has
kept the it wild enough for anyone's taste. There are still plenty of
moose, wolves, and bear thriving in the area, and the great stands
of pine are evidence of what much more of the state must have
looked like, before logging cleared much of the landscape.

But the land here is just an afterthought. Look at a map
of the region and you'll see water, water everywhere, with the
land often just a thin strip between lakes and rivers. That land is
rock, the Canadian Shield of solid granite that covers most of
the area west of Lake Superior. When the glaciers melted, the
rocky surface held the water, forming eventually the hundreds
of individual lakes, and these two, rock and water, are the base

of everything here. It took eons for plants to take hold, and more eons for something like a layer of duff to form that could support a forest. Dig just a few inches into most of that landscape, and you will hit rock. Tree roots have worked their way into the cracks in rock, and cling tenaciously to it, but the whole of earth and trees is just a thin cap over the rock itself.

And around it all is water, or rather it, the land, is only an occasional interruption in what was once one great lake. The natural way to travel here is by boat, only crossing the land to get to more water. It's still possible to follow the route of the voyageurs, those amazing Frenchmen and metis who carried fur and trade goods in their twenty-five-foot canoes from Lake Superior to Lake Athabasca, jogging across miles of portage with 180-pound loads on their backs, then paddled all day long to reach their destinations while the brief summer lasted.

To me the voyageurs are the true western heroes. They were the first real explorers of the far West, and years before other white men made the "discoveries" of western rivers and passages, these tough, colorful canoe men were using their canoe routes regularly to bring out furs and bring in trade goods for the HBC (Here Before Christ, as the Hudson's Bay Company was irreverently called). I often wonder if this country's whole history and culture might not have been improved had we taken the voyageurs as our national heroes instead of the frontiersman and cowboy. Although they were certainly as courageous and independent as the cowboy, and given to drink and brawling as well, they were also family men, fiercely protective of their women and children, and also of their relatives. They mixed freely with the Indians, and indeed intermarried until the metis often carried a complex mix of nationality, tribe and race, and they made no claims of sovereignty on the land (although the trading companies of course fought for territory). They were at least as colorful, and in a good-natured, companionable way: they loved singing and dancing, and the company of their friends and relatives, were far more generous, and even their fights were more often the outlet for high spirits rather than the territorial grudges of the later gunfighters. I sometimes think we might be a better nation had we taken the colorful, high-spirited, laughing, singing voyageurs as our heroes instead of the mean-spirited and quarrelsome frontiersmen and cowboys who followed them. Instead of trying to possess the land and wring it dry, perhaps we too would have traveled through it and lived on it with less contention and more tolerance and certainly more joy as did those first colorful travelers to the West.

Today, for most of us, the travel is more leisurely, and the goal is fishing, but along the way is some of the most beautiful lake country in the world, with little of humankind visible except the occasional fishing camp, and it's still possible to portage in to places where you'll see no one else for days. The country here is generally as flat as the water, and a good map and compass are absolute essentials even in the most-traveled areas. The shoreline is rugged, usually broken rock dropping into deep cold water, and beyond that is pine, mile after mile of green that goes from horizon to horizon. Even following a map it's sometimes hard to tell where one bay ends and the lake itself begins again, and finding a little-used portage can be a tricky venture.

Go into the BWCA from the Gunflint Trail, up big Lake Saganaga, or further east head in to Lake Namakan or Kabetogama, or from Ely start in to Burntside Lake. Wherever you begin you can travel miles and miles to ever more remote lakes, and imagine yourself in another century, where the only reminder of the modern world may be a vapor trail somewhere on the horizon. Even the modern boundaries begin to blur: one moment you may be in Minnesota, and the next you're in Canada, and there will be no real difference that you can see. (You will, however, want to check in with Canadian Customs if you're heading north, if only for your own safety—and to make sure you're fishing legally.) After the formalities, however, the two countries become one in the vast network of lake and pine country.

Fishing here, as anywhere, is a combination of knowledge and luck. There are big northern, walleyes, a fine smallmouth bass fishery (largely ignored) and some trout lakes as well, but finding them in this sprawling wilderness can be a challenge. You can hire a guide, of course, and go no further than Saganaga to fill a stringer with fat walleyes, or you can simply trust your own instincts and fish bays and weed edges that appear likely spots. Below a waterfall or rapids is almost always good for walleyes, fishing with jigs.

Northern pike are ubiquitous, but I've had my best luck trolling small bays just along the weed line. Bass too like the weeds, but you can also catch them casting or trolling along steep shoreline, where rock plunges straight down into the water, or along islands or bars.

Fishing here is a total wilderness experience, though. Once in the BWCA for a few days and you are literally in another world. "Home" becomes whatever campsite you've chosen, or the next one that you won't reach until sunset, and most of the day is spent on the water, with pine forests and rocky bluffs nearby, but mostly it's water, and when you reach camp it takes a few minutes to get used to solid ground again. The campfire takes the place of the TV, and preparing meals is a more leisurely process. If you've been lucky, there are fish to clean and then filets in the frying pan, while the coffee water boils next to the fire. The air is as clear and cold as the lakes, and redolent with pine. Stars appear in numbers you will not see in the city, and if you're lucky there will be a loon to serenade you. Occasionally you'll get duets, or whatever they are: a pair of loons performing runs and trills and weird reedy phrases, one after the other or intertwining. It's one of the most beautiful and strange performances you'll ever hear, and may go on for minutes or half an hour, after which the silence becomes even more profound. Even more occasionally there'll be a wolf howl in the distance, or a chorus, again strangely beautiful but less joyous and playful. Even in groups there's a kind of loneliness in the wolf howl, almost a lament that leaves you too feeling a little lost and alone. It's a time, late at night, for thinking long thoughts and at the same time being glad to be where you are.

The major factor in life here is the weather, and it can make you change any plans you've made in a hurry. That's part of the charm of the place, of course. You're not entirely in control, and you must be as adaptable as the rest of the creatures here. Rain in the BWCA can go on for days, and there's nothing to be done about it but curl up with a good book and listen to the spatter on the tent. It can also blow you off the lake in a hurry, as storms seem to sweep across the lake country at top speed. It's another of the delights of the place, watching the swollen clouds scud by, seemingly at tree-top level, but it's best observed from camp, and not from the boat.

When it ends, the change is quick. Sunlight dries the water from the rock, and turns the air even more pungent. The lake may take longer to quiet, but now you can sit on a log in the sun and watch it do its work.

FISH HAVE
BEAUTIFUL HOMES II

THE OTHER FISH-HOME WE ALSO SHARE in Minnesota is the southeast corner of the state, the "driftless area" missed by the glaciers as they rumbled across the northland. It is an entirely different topography and ecology, but also beautiful, and home to a different species and style of fishing. This is the "bluff country" of the Mississippi River Valley, and a region where quick little streams and rivers have cut up the limestone into a maze of ridges and valleys, unlike the vast flat lakeland to the north. It is rugged terrain, covered with a mix of deciduous and evergreen, as well as grasses and splashes of wildflowers of all kinds. It's a perfect home to birdlife, with plentiful seedplants, trees and water, and also to plentiful wildlife, including one of the richest deer herds in the state and turkeys by the hundreds; this was the first place the big birds were reintroduced in the state, and they have gone forth and multiplied prodigiously. It's also home to coyotes and the one area in the state where rattlesnakes live; the timber rattler is native here, but so reclusive it's very rarely seen.

My favorite streams in Bluff Country are the several branches of the little Whitewater River. We've camped in that area for forty years, and now keep an old Airstream on the North Branch. Just behind our trailer the river makes a bend, and there are two concrete slabs that form bridges just above water level. In very high water, sometimes both slabs are under water, making an island of the little Fairwater campground, and we try not to get caught there. It's not dangerous, as the water usually goes down soon, but it could mean a few days of isolation.

Usually, the river—and the Middle or Main Branch, and South Branch—are small, clear streams, easily wadeable and stocked with lots of rainbow and browns. Most are small, although a few grow to nine- and ten-pound monsters. It's possible because there are lots of deep holes, and also lots of places that are difficult of access. If you follow the North Branch upstream from our camp the trail peters out in a few miles, and it's all woods and a difficult climb from there on.

Not that this is wilderness, like the great northland. This area was one of the first settled in the state, and our camp is on the site of the village of Fairwater, going back to the early days of the state. Norwegians, Germans, and a few Luxembourgers staked their claims, first on the rich flat land flowing to the west, and for late-comers smaller plots in the valleys and river bottoms below. Climb up on the bluff where the land flattens into section-size fields, and the houses and barns grow in proportion to the land. Here there are large neat homes, with multiple silos and outbuildings, and the big equipment needed to farm hundreds of acres. They are post-card-perfect examples of the pastoral—and not nearly as interesting as the rugged breaks they overlook. Those who have survived carve fields anywhere they can along the ridges and strips of bottomland along the streams, plowing and planting with old eight- or nine-N Fords, running a few milking cows, and planting huge gardens beside their small houses and barns. It is a little like stepping into the Ozark Hills in some places, or back a hundred years. Many who live far back on the twisting ridge roads no longer try to farm, but make their living with cottage industries of all kinds; or simply work in one of the nearby towns.

There are a few small towns here, and most of them are farming towns. Rochester is the nearest city, about twenty miles from the Whitewaters, but then there are Plainview and St. Charles, both busy agricultural centers. Then there are Rolling-stone, in its own beautiful valley, almost to the Mississippi, and

Altura, on the eastern bluff of the Whitewater valley. The only small town right in the river bottom is Elba, at the confluence of the Main (Middle), North and South branches of the Whitewater. It's becoming a mix—there is still some farm business, from those small farms back in the valleys, but its also building a tourist business. No, it doesn't have lots of cutesy shops with antiques and souvenirs, but it does serve the basics: food, drink, and outdoor equipment are available here at a restaurant, two bars also serving food, and the Elba Express, which sells everything from gas and oil to eggs and milk to waders, turkey calls, and hunting and fishing licenses.

There are also some rooms and cabins for rent, but most of the travelers to Elba are campers. Whitewater State Park, just two or three miles up Highway 74 from Elba, has hundreds of campsites along the Main Branch of the river, and Carley, ten miles away, has a few more. There are several private campgrounds as well for "seasonals" like us, or overnighters. All are packed on the weekends all summer, and fairly busy in the spring and fall hunting seasons. Even in winter a few hardy souls come in, because there's a winter catch-and-release trout season beginning January 1st.

This is a kind of magical place, as more and more people are discovering. First of all, it's gorgeous, in a different way from other parts of the state. The Mississippi cuts its great swath just to the east, with high bluffs and a valley rich in wildlife. It's a gathering-place for eagles in their migrations, and a playground for boaters and fishermen. On either side, Wisconsin and Minnesota, smaller rivers have carved their own valleys in the limestone, creating this wrinkled and rugged landscape. It's wooded with pine and birch, oak, maple, cottonwoods of course, and because it's always damp. In summer it's a thick tangle of greener.

Before that, the wildflowers have a chance, and spring here is full of bloom and perfume. Little Carley State Park has its moment in the sun: here the bluebells carpet acres and acres, in the woods, along the river, on the hills. For a few weeks in May visitors wander through a literal sea of blue blossoms. Even before this, the bloodroot, violet, and trillium appear, less showy but delicate and persistent. And soon there are splashes of lillies, violets, lupine, and spotted touch-me-nots, lining the roads and filling the woods.

In early or mid-May too the morels appear, and this brings crowds of 'shroom lovers to Elba for the annual Morel Festival. The moist valleys are ideal for this delicious fungus, and hunters swarm from one end of the valley to another, returning to favorite spots or seeking new grounds. They're brought into Elba in bags, boxes, bushel baksets, and you can buy some fresh if you don't want to scramble up and down the hillsides.

Also in very early spring the turkey hunters arrive. Minnesota has a lottery for turkey hunting. Individuals or parties apply for one of six seasons, each lasting five days. Early seasons are usually best, as the toms are searching for hens and responding well to calls and decoys, but for that reason they're also most popular, and chances of getting a license are less than in the later seasons. This was the area turkeys were first reintroduced in the state, and the Whitewater's rugged terrain was perfect for the big birds: you can see them and hear them everywhere in the valley, although getting close enough to a big tom for a shot is another matter.

There's a second, fall season that was just introduced a few years ago, but in the fall the bow hunters are also out and about, and there are lots of deer in the valleys. I've had them wade across the creek within fifty feet of me; apparently a fly rod is not as scary as a bow and arrow.

All three branches of the Whitewater have fish, and each has different regulations. Many stretches are catch-and-release only, but there's also lots of "open" water, and the methods used for taking fish vary from corn and cheese baits to spinners to flies. It's not a purist's paradise except for those portions set aside for fly-only fishing. The DNR stocks regularly in the summer, and word spreads quickly. Meat fishermen quickly line the banks where the truck has "dumped" and pull in lots of hatchery-dumb trout. Still, there's lots of carryover, and stream counts show plenty of fish per mile on all the branches.

All the Whitewater branches are small, twenty-five to thirty feet across on average, and in most places they flow in narrow channels with lots of trees and heavy brush on the edges. Casting, therefore, can be tricky. I most often use a seven- or seven-and-one-have-foot rod, both for ease of casting and because I like the play of even a small fish on a light rod. Out of habit, probably, these are usually the rods I use fishing larger rivers as well, unless I really need to make long casts. It just takes a little longer to play out a fish, and that's half the fun anyway.

And there are some good fish here. I've had evenings with a good hatch going that have brought me six to a dozen browns from fourteen to eighteen inches, and only had to quit because the light was gone. That's admittedly rare, and usually quite early in the season; but even in mid-summer I almost always pick up a fish or two.

Throughout the season I give the Rio Grande King a workout. If they're hitting anything, or sometimes when there are no rises showing at all, I'll get some action from this all-purpose fly. Later, of course, there are hatches that call for caddis or Light Cahills or other entirely different patterns, and in late summer hoppers will get some nice fish.

The bluff country is simply a place to fish regularly, get some fish most of the time, and enjoy the moment. It's a gentle place, and easy fishing, amid some of the prettiest scenery in the country. It is not the west, but it's as close as we come in Minnesota to great trout country—a kind of miniature Montana, and a thousand miles closer.

Oh—and it also has no mosquitoes to speak of. Now in a state that flaunts the mosquito as the state bird, this is unique. No one has been able to explain it completely—perhaps the running water, perhaps the bats that inhabit the caves in the region, maybe the abundant bird life—or all three, or something else no one can explain, but it is miraculous. Here one can actually eat supper outdoors of an evening, whereas almost anywhere else in the state this would amount to suicide. Even if it were not such a lovely home for the fish, it would be worth the trip we make many times a summer just to have respite from the swarms of blood-sucking little buzzers that take over at dusk in the rest of the state.

THE PLACES
FISH LIVE II:
THE BIG HORNS

For years I've driven to Missoula as the mecca for my western fishing. A few times Anne and I took Highway 14 out of Sheridan up over the Big Horns, just for variety, and we'd stop "up top," usually at the Prune Creek campground right on the highway, sometimes spending a couple of nights just to see the moose and deer come into camp. It was a pretty drive, but we thought of it as little more than a speed-bump on the way to the more desirable fisheries.

It's an impressive bump, of course. From Sheridan 14 turns west to Dayton, then climbs quickly to almost 10,000 feet. Then there's four or five miles of flatland on top, and at Burgess Junction the highway splits. The quickest route is down to Lovell on Highway 14 itself, but it's also one of the most precipitous drops downhill in the West. When I've been towing a trailer, or even an RV with a drag-along Geo Tracker behind it, I've often taken the second route, 14A, which descends more gradually into Shell, Wyoming. The only problem with that is that, then you're in Shell, and must either find your way up north again, or go on through Yellowstone and then north. It's a longer route, but was a nice change from the interstate all the way

That five miles at the top is forest and grazing land, and although it was fun to see the wildlife, we seldom lingered in our westering. I think it was on the way home from one Missoula trip that we decided to spend a few more nights in the Bighorns. We weren't ready to leave the mountains yet, and this is the last real western range, although the Black Hills are a close imitation farther down the road. At the Prune Creek campground I'd fished once or twice for the plentiful brookies, and now we wandered off to other creeks in the area. When one begins traveling the spine of the Big Horns south and north, there's a lot more country than can be seen from Highway 14, and we crisscrossed the back roads on each side of the highway, fishing small streams at Tie Flume and Dead Swede campgrounds, which were also full of eager little brookies.

I'd almost overlooked what turned out to be the jewel of Big Horn fishing, aside from the Big Horn itself which is on the west side of the mountains and is primarily a float-fishing river. The Tongue River runs right along Highway 14 on the top of the mountains, and then drops east into Ranchester, and there's some excellent fishing down at the lower end. On the top, though, is some great fun. It's catch and release, but there are large cutthroat everywhere. In one short run, the water was literally boiling with feeding fish—a cliché I know—but I've never seen it actually happening. It didn't matter what fly I used particularly, just so it was very small, and I'd get a hit almost every cast. In a half hour, I connected with about a dozen fish in the fourteen- to eighteen-inch range, and finally just quit at dark, although the water was still churning.

This was intriguing enough to keep us in the Big Horns a week, and although it didn't happen every evening, I did hit similar hatches a number of times, in various spots. The only hazard along this stretch is that it's a moose haven, and I found myself looking over my shoulder frequently. They're usually gentle beasts, but they are unpredictable and they're big, and when I spotted one I always felt more comfortable moving to some other spot.

Even in the little Prune Creek campgrounds, just off Highway 14, there were moose in camp regularly, and in the evening Anne and I often just drove the byways looking for the big critters. And dodging the deer, which are as thick as the trout. We lost count, even driving on 14, of the whitetails wandering along the road and pastures.

Over the years, we've made the Big Horns a regular detour, and found them enchanting. The wildlife in itself is amazing. In addition to moose and deer, we've seen herds of fifty or more elk, and beautiful bulls wandering just off the highway. Although bear are not plentiful, I did run into a pair far down a little creek on the south side of the mountain—fortunately at some distance—and I did a quick about-face without them even spotting me, but it was a rare bit of good luck to see them at all.

Off the highway, it is rugged country. Most of the back roads are closed, and there's snow well into June in the high elevations. And it is high, with peaks running over 13,000 feet. There's lots of real wilderness, roadless areas and massive ridges, some of it accessible by horseback, and also some tourist attractions: on the branch of Highway 14 going to Shell is Antelope Butte Ski Area, and there are cross-country trails laid out as well. The Medicine Wheel on Alternate 14 to Lovell is amazing, and draws native Americans from all over, who still consider it one of the great holy places of the West. For the tourist, it's spectacular. And if you're not used to the altitude, the mile-long hike at 10,000 feet plus is a challenge.

There is a tourist center just as you reach the top of the mountains coming from the east, and we've found them very helpful. They not only have maps and books on the area, but the people at the center have explored most of it personally, so they can guide you to wildlife concentrations and attractions not always noted in the guidebooks. Up on the flat top of the mountain are a couple of lodges, and gas and other supplies are available, although telephones are a problem. There are phones available, but in our experience they're not at all reliable, and you're generally off the cell-phone zone as well.

Now the Big Horns are one of our primary destinations, especially if we don't feel like making the long drive to Missoula. In itself it has spectacular mountain scenery, the best wildlife viewing of any place I know, outside the big parks, and some fine fishing. Also, because of the short summer season and its distance off the interstate, there are seldom many tourists and/or fishermen in the Horns, and your neighbors are more often four-footed or hooved than human.

 # THE PLACES
FISH LIVE III:
THE GALLATIN

PPR: In summer 2005 Anne and I stopped as usual at the Castle Rock cabins and campgrounds on the Gallatin River. We weren't sure if Fred Weschenfelder, the longtime owner of the place, would be there or not. The year before he'd been in agony from chronic back problems, and had thought he might have to give up the place, but he said he'd had surgery in Billings and was about ninety percent recovered—amazing, because he'd seen specialists all over, and not given much chance of improvement.

We caught up on his news in the café with the old bullet-hole in one wall. He claimed his ex-wife really hadn't wanted to hit him, because she was a dead shot; if she'd wanted to she would surely have nailed him, which had always made him feel better. In both cases, we were glad he was still there and that the place was in operation. The cabins aren't fancy, but they are clean and comfortable and have, really, all the conveniences one could want, including kitchens. Although we'd often parked a trailer or RV there as well, this year we were just traveling in our Outback wagon, staying in motels or cabins: at the price of gas, we'd decided this was as economical as running the RV for two or three thousand miles on our annual trip west, and in some ways more convenient: we didn't have to "shop" for a campground, or for parking room every time we went into town for something.

Castle Rock is about twenty miles down the Gallatin from Bozeman, on a nice stretch of fishing water and convenient to more good fishing in either direction, down to Gallatin Gateway and upstream to Yellowstone. After Rock Creek, it's the river I've fished most in Montana. It's not just one of the best rivers I know of, but also one of the most beautiful.

Except for a few places, though, it's not an easy stream to fish. Other than the upper river, which meanders through relatively flat terrain out of Yellowstone, the Gallatin is one series of rapids after another, through big jutting rocks and narrow chutes with a few stretches of deep holes. Raft fishing is popular, and there's also plenty of access for wading, but both are a little tricky. The water is a beautiful light green, very cold, and in many places drops off quickly where the channel is cut through solid rock.

I was reminded of that dramatically the second day of fishing on this trip. We'd finished supper, and I didn't feel like driving anywhere, so I climbed down the steep bank just downstream from our cabin, where there's a stretch of relatively flat water below some rapids. Even there, the current is strong enough so you can only wade out about twenty feet from shore. Then it's hip-deep, and there's current enough to make anything more pretty treacherous. No one else was in sight, and I was casting from there into deeper water, around rocks that made nice barriers and often held feeding fish behind them. I'd been at it for only a few minutes when I heard someone shouting, but the voice was muffled and I couldn't see anyone nearby. Then I looked a little farther upriver, and across. At first I thought it was someone fishing from that side, except that he didn't have any equipment, and indeed, when I moved up a little more, I could see that he didn't have any clothes either.

He was far enough away so I couldn't see him clearly, but obviously he was not where he ought to be, and not dressed for wandering the river bank. I hollered back, and could finally make out a feeble, "Help," call, so I told him to stay put and I started up to the camp. I found Fred in the café, and soon there was a small crowd keeping an eye on the man, who was now more obviously in distress. He would stand up and take a few faltering steps, then collapse to sitting again.

There was no way to get a rope across, or for anyone to wade; the rapids just below the cabins are fierce, and there's a deep fast channel on the other side. Fred sent a younger man up to the next bridge, about a quarter mile up the road, and in fifteen or twenty minutes we spotted him scrabbling along the steep bank on the other side. He got the man on his feet, and then started back up the hill with the other hanging on to his belt and stumbling up the slope.

Somehow they managed to get back to a car, and covered him with blankets and poured hot coffee in him. Back at Castle Rock he told us which cabin he was in, and we put him to bed. He was very pale and shivering, just on the brink of hypothermia; but it looked as if he'd be okay.

In the meantime his partner showed up, more or less as part of the crowd. He was by contrast very red-faced, and very boozy. He mumbled out the story: they'd been wading about a half-mile upstream, and his partner had tried to get out to a rock in mid-current where he could fish some good water. Even sober it would have been tough, and in his shape he was bounced downstream, clothes ripping off on the rocks, until the current washed him up where I spotted him.

Supposedly drunks will survive car crashes that should kill them because they're relaxed and limp; things don't break as easily. That must have been true here, because although the man had lots of bruises and abrasions, and was nearly in shock, there were no other serious injuries. What nearly killed him was that he sat naked on the bank of the Gallatin for almost an hour, after being flung downriver in icy water for a half mile. Why his partner didn't raise the alarm right away was a mystery, except that both of them were very drunk. He apparently also froze, and just couldn't figure out what to do.

By morning they were both up and around, but they left that day, probably embarrassed to be seen around the camp, and I hope a little wiser about river fishing and about the Gallatin in particular. People do drown in it regularly, and I've become even more cautious after watching this near miss first hand.

The danger is what gives it its beauty, of course. That light-green water churns and swirls around great rocks, and roars through tight channels, then spreads into deep pools. Even there the water is moving, rolling, pulling everything inexorably down. In those pools and along the edges of the ripping water and behind rocks there are trout, lots of them, and although they're fished heavily, they will hit a dry fly readily. They hit fast, per-haps because the water is continually and everywhere moving, and they must catch their meals on the run. Once caught, they are into the current and running. Getting them into the net is a real challenge. I hooked my first twenty-inch-plus brown on a stretch of fairly calm water just above a roaring rapids, and spent half an hour scrambling along the bank to keep up with the running fish. I did land him, without a Brad Pitt-like ride down the river, but he'd run most of the line off my reel at one point before suddenly surging back up-stream where I could work him to the bank.

Even access to the water is often difficult, since the Gallatin has steep banks almost everywhere, and often those banks simply continue to drop. The only way to fish is from the land, meaning the bank is behind you and there's little room for back casts. Sometimes it's possible to work out the line parallel to the bank, hold-ing the rod straight out, then on the last back throw "shooting" straight out. More often a roll cast will get the line out far enough to reach fishable water. There are places one can wade, but again the river is built on big rocks, and a sudden misstep can suddenly put you in deep stuff, and you can end up with wet feet at best, or a quick ride down the river.

There are plenty of access points, but they too pres-ent a peculiarly modern hazard. Unlike my favorite Rock Creek, which has a bumpy, lightly traveled road along its length, the Gallatin has U.S. Highway 191 beside it all the way from Gallatin Gateway to Yellow-tone Park, and it's a smooth, fast two-lane blacktop all the way, and it is full of high-speed traffic at all hours. The development of the Big Sky complex upriver has increased the traffic even more, and besides tourists and residents, there are trucks of all kinds barreling along its length. The highway builders have done their best: there are pull-outs frequently, and often at good fishing areas, but darting into them from a line of seventy-mile-per-hour traffic is often suicidal. Many of the pull-outs have black skid-marks where fishermen have "landed" after leaving the traffic, sort of like hitting a short runway and hoping you'll stop before the tarmac runs out. It's not exactly the pristine wilderness one would prefer, but it does provide plenty of opportunities to get on the river.

For all the challenge, it's worth it. There are good hatches regularly in the deep valley of the river, and of course you'll want to try to match the caddis or duns when the fish are rising regularly, but it's also one of the few rivers where fish will take attractors when there's no big hatch coming off. I've had great success here with the Royal Wulff and Trude, fishing around the rocks and even in fast runs. Those classic Coachman patterns have, frankly, seldom worked for me elsewhere, but for some reason the big browns of the Gallatin are especially partial to them. They are selective, but when they're hitting the Gallatin trout are, like the river, fast and wild, and it's exciting to see them coming up out of the clear deep water. You'll often see them coming ten feet away, and it's a challenge to hold off until they've actually hit. I've even had them skitter across the current after a fly—and I've also had them make equally quick decisions not to hit that particular offering just at the last second.

The traffic and the upstream development are unfortunate, but so far they have not had much effect on the river itself. It's still one of the great blue-ribbon streams in the west, and certainly one of the most beautiful.

 # THE PLACES
FISH LIVE IV:
A SELECTED LIST

Reader: Yes, I have to agree that one of the joys of fishing is that it takes you to beautiful places, and you've picked out some of the most scenic settings and beautiful rivers in the West, and they're all good fishing rivers. However, they're also all pretty well known, and you promised early on that you would give up a few "secret places" just to make the book worth buying.

PPR: Well, I thought the Tongue River in the Big Horns was enough of a secret place to fulfill that promise. Do I have to give everything away? Every fisherman ought to have places no one else knows about.

Reader: Come on! You've given away almost nothing that every other fisherman doesn't know about.

PPR: But this section was to be about aesthetics, about the gentle surround, and not so much about the fishing—which is, also, superb in all the places I mentioned. I see no reason to give up all my secrets, or pretty soon everyone will be fishing them and they won't be secret or mine any more.

Reader: Okay, you have a point there. You could at least, though, list a few of the other good—and beautiful—rivers you've fished, and maybe slip in one that's "special." Then the reader—me—will at least have to figure out which is the best of the best, and since most of us don't have time to fish everything, chances are only a few will stumble across your favorite.

PPR: That makes sense to me, although my list will be more limited. I haven't fished anywhere near all the rivers in the West, but I'll list a few that have been productive, including one or two that are really magnificent—even if they're not among the big-name, blue-ribbon streams. That should keep anyone busy, and if they do hit on the really good ones, why more power to them. Most of those are underfished anyway, and a few more fishermen won't affect the fishing much. If you want really comprehensive lists of trout fishing in Montana, browse through John Holt's *Montana Fly Fishing Guide,* in two volumes for east and west Montana. Exploring all the streams listed there would take several lifetimes.

So here goes my abbreviated list. These are some streams I've fished that have ranged from mediocre to stupendous, with brief commentary:

The Big Blackfoot near Missoula, the "home river" for Norman MacLean's characters in *A River Runs through It,* is no longer quite so rich in fish as during his youth. Silver mining upstream seriously damaged the trout population over a period of years, and it's only recently that restrictions have improved the water quality. Now the Blackfoot is making a real comeback, and if the polluters can be held at bay, may again become one of the great blue-ribbon streams of Montana.

In the same area around Missoula are the Jocko, the Clarks Fork itself, the Bitterroot, and several of its tributaries. Lolo Creek is one of the best of these.

Heading east again from Missoula, you'll cross the Little Blackfoot River, a small easily wadeable stream full of big browns. It's very narrow in places, and you have to slam a fly in close to the willows along the edges, but there are some startlingly big fish there.

Further down the road, around Big Timber, is the Boulder River. It's a bit like a small-scale Gallatin: rocky, sometimes hard to wade, but not so dangerous. Fish are plantiful, and occasionally there are big ones in the deeper holes and runs.

Other big rivers in Montana include the Madison, the Flathead, the Big Hole, the Big Horn, and the Yellowstone itself, all of which are best fished by floating. All the larger rivers have smaller spring stream tributaries, which often provide faster action than the big waters, but fewer really huge fish.

Yellowstone Park and Glacier have many fine streams, of course. Some are heavily fished, but they're well stocked, and if you're willing to hike there are plenty of relatively "wild" streams further off the road

The only river I've fished in Wyoming, aside from the Big Horns, is the Wind River. This is again a big river, but has huge browns and lots of cutthroat in it. I've done well just casting from shore, although the current in most places is a problem. Again, this is a better river for float fishing.

And then there's all of Idaho, with the fabled Henry's Fork, Silver Creek, and St. Joe River, and a total of ten world-class blue-ribbon streams. I haven't fished Idaho enough to give any sound advice based on my own experience, but I've talked to other fishermen who have found Idaho every bit as good as Montana, if a little more limited in the number of streams available.

Wherever you go on these streams, the fishing should be at least satisfactory, although trout fishing is never a sure thing. What is guaranteed is that you'll be in beautiful country, with clear cold water and mountains and redolent forests everywhere. Like any trip, it's not the destination but the getting there that's often more important; and although fish may be the target for this kind of travel, the rewards may come as much from being in the beautiful places where trout make their homes.

THE FISHERMAN SURVIVES WINTER IN MINNESOTA

Reader: I'm new to Minnesota, as well as to fishing, and this, my first summer, was paradise. I fished dawn to dusk (when I wasn't reading your treatise), and even reached a sort of understanding with my wife, thanks to your advice.

And then, the apocalypse! In late fall, all the water froze, the trees died, the roads became icy trails to nowhere. All of Minnesota became a frozen lump, the fish were shielded by three feet of ice, and even leaving the house became Survival 101. Now my wife, left alone all summer, is screaming at me to "Go somewhere. Take a trip. Get out of thehouse," a subtle hint that fishermen are like drone bees, and once their function is served, they should go elsewhere.

PPR: Ah, the realities of Minnesota, Paradise Lost for Half the Year, have struck you. As a native myself, and having survived many a winter here, in Piscus Interruptus, as it were, I can again offer both solace—and some practical advice.

First, do go elsewhere. Montana's fishing season is open all year. Other temperate climes offer freshwater or saltwater angling in the Minnesota's Season of Despair.

Reader: Whoa! Maybe once, but I've already spent a fortune on fishing tackle. The wife won't travel in the winter, and going to Mexico for a month—well, I'd lose my job, be flat broke, and I'm quite sure my wife would not be here when I go back. So scratch that.

PPR: In my profession one solution is to get a grant—to study Hemingway's writing habits in Key West, or Cuba, or anyplace else he actually wrote, while spending much of the day chasing sailfish. Easy enough to justify experiencing his whole routine, without spending overmuch time at a desk. Lately, that only works a few times before the slim scholarly returns fail to impress the dean. And I know that's probably not open to you, having chosen the wrong profession for a fisherman. You'll just have to live with that, and there are other options.

You can buy a fishing shack, perhaps half the size of your house, a bigger truck to haul it, install a killer audio/TV system, kitchen and wet bar, and join the armies who head for those frozen lakes at the first sign of frost. You may have to mortgage your house, but if you don't drive through the ice at some point you can spend as much time away from home as in summer.

Do not misunderstand, however—this is not fishing, although that's the rationale for it all. Ice fishing is simply another culture completely, and while the participants dutifully cut holes in the ice and drop lines into the void below, the real purpose of this madness is primarily social. There are few lone ice fishermen. There indeed are hardy souls, serious die-hard fishermen, who tend their lines as attentively as they would a trolling rod in summer. For most, though, ice-fishing is an excuse to play cards, drink beer, eat all the jerky and junk food they can bring, and enjoy the camaraderie of hundreds of other winter-crazed and bored Minnesotans. They may be occasionally interrupted by a pesky pike, which is usually simply thrown outside on the ice until they want to deal with it.

There is no denying that ice-fishing has its attractions, but it should not be confused with real fishing and is a feeble substitute for it. To the dedicated fisherman, those who believe fishing should focus on catching fish and be conducted only in water that is liquid, there are other options, but they're best saved up until those last desperate days when fifty-degree days give way to another week of subzero and snow, when you've watched all the old movies you can stand, and when all you want is to think fishing, to get your fishing fix.

For me, the first year, those reflections brought back the memory of a last bass trip I'd taken that had ended with a snarled line on my best spinning outfit, so that was a natural starting point. I'd simply put it away for the season, just the way it was, and the old Mitchell 300 was not only snarled but needed all new line. Monofilament does last a long time, but it gets weak spots, and after a season with the normal number of snarls, it also gets too short on the reel to cast well. For any of these reasons, it's a good time to run to the local tackle store—where of course one thing will lead to another, and you'll have spent another cold day in comfort, in your natural environment—and also probably spent a bit of cash on the shiny new toys that are brought forth each season, "guaranteed to catch fish," "outlawed in Colorado," yeah, that sort of thing. One day in the fisherman's candy store is delightful, and useful, and probably enough: it can be habit-forming.

So you've finally come back home with the new, extra-limp, invisible-to-fish mono, and possibly a few other trophies. (They can be smuggled in, in a brown paper grocery bag, or easily hidden in the voluminous folds of a winter coat.) The next step is to disappear into your basement or study. Your wife will not know or care where you are, just that you're gone (it's been a long winter for her too, remember).

Once surrounded by fishing gear, one thing will lead to another. After replacing suspect lines, it's also a good idea to check on the action in all your reels. Most are not that difficult to break down, and a little gear grease, Vaseline, or WD-40 (and some cleaning) will make the next summer's fishing a lot better.

Then of course you should check rods as well. There isn't as much to go wrong here, other than outright breakage or a need to upgrade (back to the tackle store, if you dare), but it is worth looking over the reel seat and handle, making sure everything's tight, and then looking more closely at the guides. If they're nicked or beginning to show wear, it might be time to use a file or emery cloth on them, or replace them. Pay special attention to the tip-top. That usually wears most and can cut into a line quickly. If you must replace it, try pulling it off, with a little heat if necessary. However, they can be infernally stubborn, and eventually clipping off the tip may be the only solution. Losing that quarter-inch won't make that much difference in the action of most rods, and it's better than a line that begins to shred at some critical point.

The biggest and most time-consuming job is the tackle boxes and fishing vests. I realized once I got into my own tackle-storage systems that it had been several seasons since I'd really gone through everything. Besides being pretty foul, things were pretty seriously cluttered and tangled—and in no particular order any longer. The only solution was to take everything out and start fresh, and while it was out, cleaning the box(es) and vests. If you're really going to be systematic, you should next do a little planning before dumping everything back in: most-used items on the top shelf, scales and filet knives, and extra reels in the bottom— whatever works for you.

And you'll probably find as I did that the terminal tackle (hooks, sinkers, snap swivels, leaders, and so on) are all over the place. I used some small plastic boxes— pill boxes, small fly boxes, as well as the original sinker and hook containers) to sort things out and keep everything contained. It may not last long, but at least you can start the season knowing where everything is.

Then I started through the lures. Since I fish everything from bass and pike to sunfish and river cats, I have a little of everything. That's desirable, but over the years, when I couldn't find what I wanted, or just admired something new, it often went in the tackle box anywhere there was space. As a result, I found I had at least a dozen Rapalas, from floating to Shad Raps, somewhere in there, and duplicates and triplicates of many others. I ended up with a separate box for spares, which I can use to replace one of the several I still kept, together, in one compartment.

Check over each lure. The old Hula Popper may need a new skirt, or others a good cleaning and some repair. If the hooks are rusty on a favorite old Lazy Ike, this is the time to invest in some new treble hooks. Or if it's also battered beyond redemption, you could (horrors!) throw it away. Better yet, find another box—a memory box, if you will, for "retired" lures. I'd bet you can still remember a big bass hitting that old Flatfish, and some future winter you can relive it again.

I also found a surplus of spare line, disgorgers, scales, knives, pliers and screwdrivers, multi-tools, and other equipment along with the lures, and although I carry a large tackle box, all of it was not necessary, or at least not several of each. Getting out the extras not only made things better organized and convenient, but lightened the box considerably.

Fly vests present some of the same problems, and some new ones. There was unnecessary equipment there as well, but the big problem is always the flies. Trout fishermen know that you can never have too many varieties of flies right there, on your person, for that fish that only wants one pattern, size, and color. At the same time, probably seventy-five percent of the time you use a half-dozen flies, of which you must have several of each. That means a vest that is probably stuffed with small boxes, Copenhagen cans, and Band-Aid tins full of flies, as well as those on the woolly patches of your vest or hat. I don't think there is a final solution to this delightful confusion, but you can at least start each season with a couple of boxes with only "old standards," in several sizes, and then a few (a couple, if you can manage it) with the infinite variety you're going to need for a particular hatch—and mark the boxes with indelible ink to save going through every pocket every time there's a new bug on the water. You'll also find, as I did, a lot of flies that are rusty, battered, or just unproductive. If you can, just dump them—yes, even that sponge-green grasshopper that looked so good but never brought a hit. By the end of the season, of course, they'll all be mixed up, here and there, or gone to a tree.

This is a good time for a little reflection as well, for memories of times and trips past. There may be too much equipment, too many lures in your tackle box. Don't of course, throw any of it away: that River Runt will be exactly what you need on the next trip. Keep a second, surplus box for things not used regularly.

And that's really the second point. As you go through, you should have been keeping a list of those things missing—starting with that second tackle box for "extras." Although you started with too many things in your box, you've now organized it and thinned it, so you have room for some essentials that are not in it. Maybe that last trip got a little dicey when the motor quit after dark, and you realized you didn't have a flashlight anywhere, or you actually didn't have a medium-running Rapala among the dozen deep and floating models in the box.

Which takes us to yet another wonderful way to pass some winter time. A trip to the local sports store for those missing essentials on your list can be a wonderful morale-booster, as well as helping you prepare. Like me, you'll probably find some new things you didn't know you couldn't live without. (I discovered a set of gadgets in several sizes called "lure-keepers," clever nylon and Velcro pockets that can be clapped around the lure, either when you take it off or while it's still on the rod. It's perfect for keeping lures from coupling or tripling in complex tangles.) They may not be new items, but they were certainly something I badly needed. I even found a good place to put them in my shiny new tackle box where I'll be able to find them, when summer comes. May it be soon!

THE GREAT
WHITE TROUT

Reader: Okay, I've survived my first Minnesota winter, thanks to your advice. My tackle is like new, my tackle box is organized and accessible. I did have to buy two more boxes to hold all the things I found in the sports stores (I ended up spending five days shopping, toward the end of February, when the cabin fever had me insane.) And when it snowed ten inches in early March, I grabbed a plane for Mexico and spent three beautiful days fishing sailfish, bonito, and tuna out of Zihuatanejo. My wife is speaking to me again, but in those clipped, snappish tones that tell me I'm very near the edge. I've been walking softly the last week or two, and have not mentioned fishing once. (I also haven't mentioned the credit card numbers I've rung up over the winter.)

And I won't for another week or two, because it's still miserable out there, the lakes are still iced over, and I think she'll come around. We did even have a sort-of conversation about my "hobby," and she did agree that I can take a few trips each summer (number not specified), as long as they're in the state.

So—when is the earliest time I can plan to get out? I've had a couple of weeks without touching my tackle box, or even looking at sports magazines, to say nothing of fishing, and I'm ready. With the lakes frozen, what are my options?

PPR: I think you're treading on thin ice, so to speak, to be planning another trip this soon after a falling out with your wife, but we've been over that, and I assume you know what you're doing.

Reader: I know, absolutely, that I have to go fishing soon or I'll go nuts. I've tried really hard, and she did say trips in-state were okay, and I'll just have to take my chances. I'm ready not just for fishing, but for a little adventure—like fishing with gloves on.

PPR: Oh, in that case I have just the thing for you. You'll not only wear gloves, but insulated waders, all the clothes you can put on, and you'll still be miserable, cold and wet most of the time. And you will probably lose most of the fish you catch.

Reader: That sounds wonderful. And why should I do this?

PPR: Because, my friend you will have a chance to catch some of the most beautiful, powerful, and best-tasting fish in the world—the steelhead trout. Now I do not urge you to do this, but you do sound close to the brink, and this at least keeps you in the state. And there are other caveats: It can become an obsession, like Captain Ahab's desire for a certain white whale, or the muskie fisherman trying year after year for that one monster pike.

It usually begins in mid-April when there's still snow in the shaded banks along the rivers of the Upper Great Lakes. What snow has already melted fills the rivers, so they thunder and roar with brown water. That water flows out into the Great Lakes, and the fish start to gather. And the fishermen.

Otherwise normal men become forgetful, develop strange habits, usually involving old boots and unusual tackle. Many are "regular" fishermen as well, though to some this is the only kind of fish worth pursuing, but all react in weird ways to the run of the steelhead.

Typically, you begin as I did last year at 4:40 a.m., stumbling down the banks of the Knife River north of Duluth, hoping to find a good spot. As I finally reached the water, and began to be able to see, dark shapes loomed out everywhere, like herons on stalks. There were fishermen every six feet, on both sides of the river, in the pitch black and icy cold. They would be there most of the day, and only total paralysis of the legs— or a complete absence of fish—would drive them off their claim.

These madmen had all converged on the Knife as if they, too, could smell the spring rush of water. Many did get more tangible signals—a phone call from a friend on the North Shore, or a call to the Chamber of Commerce in Duluth, or an item in a local paper— but many had come because they could stand it no longer, and just "felt" it was the right time.

They swarm around the rivers, pitch primitive camps or search for motel rooms. Because the lake has been open, some fish from boats around the mouths of the rivers, where the trout "stack up" before making the up-stream run. The rest of us trudge feverishly up one stream bank and then another, looking for likely spots to fish.

The run usually begins on the rivers nearest Du-luth—the south end of the North Shore—and then opens up as the warm weather moves north, until the run is on all the way to Grand Marais and beyond. Just now though most of the fishermen concentrate on the Lester, the French, the Sucker and the Knife, where the fish should be running. Usually I am among those too early or too late, but even though April 10 is a week or more ahead of the average time for the run to begin, warm weather has opened the rivers early, and the steelhead are running!

Everyone knows this by now, and each fisherman concentrates on the feel of his lure, working out there in the murky water. Suddenly someone shouts "fish!" and all the lines come in. Nets are yanked from their backsnaps by those downstream. Very often it will be someone there, rather than the fisherman himself, who nets the fish. Sometimes the man with the fish on will begin a mad dash down the river, if the fish is strong and if he's gotten into the current and if there's room to run. About half the time today there will be a fish in someone's net, a fish weighing from three or four pounds to ten, twelve or more. They are powerful, even in the net, and beautiful—sometimes almost silver, more often darker and richly colored. After the spawning, they will turn white, and the flesh of those caught returning to the lake will be softer, less desirable.

They will be easier to catch then, though. Now the big rainbows have only one thing in mind: laying the eggs that swell in their sparkling bellies. To tempt them, the trouter uses colorful foam imitations, or yarn flies, but most often spawn bags. All are "bumped" along the bottom, weighted down with sinkers so they just tick the rocks as the current carries them along. Most of the fishermen use long, heavy fly rods strung with monofilament line, the better to feel the bounce of the lure. When the bouncing stops, or when "something happens," they set the hook.

What it is that happens is part of the mystery. There is seldom a hard strike, and most often certain knowledge of the fish comes only after the hook has been set. It is done mostly by instinct.

And why the fish hit at all is another mystery, because most have nothing in their stomachs. They have not been feeding on their single-minded journey. There are theories: they hit out of anger, from being disturbed in their upstream struggle. Or they instinctively mouth the bait, even though they have no urge to feed. Or, as one angler suggested to me this year, they may be simply trying to replace spawn that has broken loose from the bottom, trying to glue it down again to help continue the species. None of these has the ring of certain truth, but one must be true because once in a while there is suddenly a fish on.

My first fish was on near the tail of a pool on the Big Sucker River, after I'd given up trying to find a place on the Knife. The Sucker is a narrow, raging stream that has good runs of fish, and terrible conditions for getting a hooked fish landed. I've lost two fish there in the last two years. This was one. He drove immediately out of the pool where I'd hooked him, downstream into a wild rush of current where I couldn't follow because of trees lining the bank. A neighbor tried to give me a hand as I held the trout briefly in the surge of water, but just as his net began its scoop, my over-strained line let go.

A word here about the very real physical dangers of steelheading. I was standing on a mix of snow and mud, the narrow trail down the bank of the Sucker, and all along the trail were birch and pine trees. The river was a few feet below me, and too deep and rocky for wading, and below the pool the current could sweep you downstream in a second. On some other rivers, you can wade in knee-deep, but even there the undertow is powerful, and a misstep can send you, waders and all, into the terrible icy river. Losing a fish is sometimes the only choice, rather than losing your life, as several do each year in the steelhead frenzy.

Losing the fish is a terrible moment, but a part of the sport and the obsession. You don't always win against the big trout, and they wouldn't be half as fascinating if it was a sure thing. I repeated this to myself as I climbed wearily out of the deep valley of the Sucker. It didn't help.

The best fishing time of the day was over. If I had taken that trout, I would have quit for the day. Instead I returned to the Knife and was still fishing at 1:00. The crowd had thinned out a little, enough to allow me a spot on the Sucker Pool, a widening of the river that is often a resting place for numbers of steelhead. There had been a number taken during the morning hours. The run was developing nicely. Now, though, there was very little action to be seen anywhere. Many of the fishermen had gone off for much needed rest and food, until evening when the run might pick up again.

And then I had another one on. It was a heavy fish. They usually "bulldog" near the bottom, and their motions, though powerful, are slower and less frantic than smaller trout. It fought hard, but the fish stayed in the pool. In a short time my downstream neighbor netted a beautiful dark eight-pound female, dripping with spawn.

Then I did quit. I spent the rest of the afternoon making up spawn bags of the fresh eggs, using pieces of nylon stocking, and dozing to make up for the short night and the day slogging through snow and mud, or standing in icy water. I fished again that evening, and was up again at 4:00 the next morning, but with no more luck, either with the crowds or the fish. At noon my weekend was over, and I started the long drive home. And despite the prospect of a 250-mile drive, and the cold, and the smell of ripe spawn and fish that would ripen further as I neared home, I knew that next year I would start the same trip again, just as surely as the steelhead would begin their journey once more.

AFTER THE GREAT
WHITE TROUT

IT IS TWO WEEKS LATER. **PPR** AND THE **READER** MEET AGAIN.

Reader: Well, that was a total disaster. Thanks for your wonderful advice, which got me exactly no fish, five days of stumbling through snow and mud in frigid water and air, and an equally frigid greeting when I got home. I don't know why I ever listen to you.

PPR: My dear sir, please remember that I cautioned you, in fact tried to discourage you, from this venture. And what do you mean, five days? You had planned to just fish two days to keep to your bargain with your wife.

Reader: (Mumbles) Well, the second day I actually had a fish on. I'd gotten on the Knife very early and found a spot, and almost immediately felt something toying with my bait, and when I struck I thought I was snagged—until the snag began moving slowly downstream. I was so surprised I didn't move, at first; and by the time I shouted "Fish" and started downstream, the fish was in the rapids. He stripped all the line from my reel and then just kept going with it, down to the lake, I suppose.

So of course I had to keep trying—I was perhaps a little excited by then—and hooked two more fish, and lost them both, and suddenly I'd been there five days, so it's not my fault, right? And would you help me explain this to my wife, who dumped all my clothes from the trip into the backyard, and will not speak to me, nor listen.

PPR: No and again no, dear sir. I might understand your reasons, but she? Never. Nor will I become involved between husband and wife. I could only deflect some of the blame, but never lessen it. You must only hope time eases her anger, and you must plead insanity and apologize profusely.

Reader: I know, I know. It's just that the regular trout season has just opened, and I don't know if I can wait for her to cool off. The best fishing on the Whitewater is now, in early summer, and I don't want to miss it.

By the way, I didn't get to the North Shore until the 15th of April. Do you think if I went up earlier next year . . . ?

PPR: Dear sir, I believe I hear my wife calling me to dinner, and she is "the one who must be obeyed." You might just keep that in mind. Good day, good sir . . . and good luck.

 # TO THE SEA

PPR: A disclaimer, at the beginning. I know very little about salt water fishing, and only began it late in life. What little I've seen, though, only shows me how much I've missed, and I want to just add it to the possibilities of a fishing life.

Like so many others, after retirement Anne and I often headed south in the winter. We've spent vacations (if you can have a vacation in retirement) in Arizona, New Mexico, Florida, the Gulf Coast of Texas, and Mexico. We soon discovered that, for us, those places on the ocean had the most appeal. To me it was almost a necessity to be near water. Most of the Southwest is desert, and although there's some fishing, it's mostly a place for golfers. I do not play golf; in fact I actively dislike golf, if only because it is such a waste of water, especially in places where water is as precious as in the Southwest.

At any rate, I needed to be someplace that offered fishing as well as warmth, and so we focused on the coastal areas of both the United State and Mexico. Now, by the time I got around to coastal fishing, I was in my sixties and mostly ignorant of saltwater tackle, fish, or methods. My first experiences were from the beaches of the Texas coast, and consisted of surf-casting and pier-fishing. I bought a monstrous rod and a spinning reel that looked like my Mitchell 300 on steroids, and I learned from kindly sportshop owners what kind of rig to use and what baits. I have managed to catch a variety of fish, from sea trout to sharks to sheepshead, plus some others I couldn't identify, and a great number of nasty little stingrays and hardhead catfish. It's good sport, and has the great advantage of a multiplicity of species: you're never sure what you'll hook, and it might be something really big. The ocean is fascinating in its complexity and almost infinite variety, and even with the most basic tackle and skills it's great sport.

I went out a few times in a boat, both in Florida and Texas, and added a few more species to my list, and a few more techniques to my repertoire. However, to me ocean fishing must ultimately mean deep-sea fishing—corrupted by Hemingway, I suppose—and it wasn't until we began going to Mexico regularly that I finally had my chance to head out into deeper water.

We discovered Zihuatanejo through some research and some luck. I wanted to go someplace in Mexico that was not an American beach compound isolated from the country itself, and not dedicated to golf, rum drinks with plastic flowers, and shopping. I read all the travel books I could find, and eventually decided that Zihuatanejo, Mexico, sounded most like what I wanted. Although it's a "twin city" with Ixapa, a government-built artificial community for Americans, Zihuat is still decidedly a Mexican fishing town. There are an increasing number of facilities for tourists, but most of the people are still Spanish-speaking and many still make their living by fishing—or by taking Americans and Canadians fishing. It was and is exactly what we wanted, and we've gone back year after year. Fortunately, it's not everyone's cup of tequila. Ixtapa is still favored by the golf-and-margarita crowd, and I hope it stays that way.

My first outings in Zihuat were in *pangas*, the small craft that most local fishermen use, and we fished around the bays and a few miles out in the deeper water. I added tuna and bonito to my list, as well as more sharks. Then eventually I found fishing partners to share the cost of a larger boat, and at last we went out twenty-plus miles, to where the big fish play. On my last visit, we hooked five sailfish over two days, and I discovered what I'd really been missing: this was serious fishing, where the fish might be nearly as big as you and where it became a matter of who wore out first.

When my first sail came out of the water, it seemed a mile away, and I couldn't believe how big it was, or how strong, or how wild and beautiful. He was a good fish, as Hemingway would say, almost nine feet long, and it took me half an hour to bring him to the boat. We were releasing all our fish, except for a bonito that we'd later have cooked up at the hotel, but I'm sorry to say my first sail had swallowed the hook, and we had to keep him. I ended up giving him to the captain of the boat, who would then sell him to one of the restaurants along the beach, so it was not a total waste, but I still felt bad about killing that magnificent fighter.

Except for that disappointment, it was a wonderful experience. The only drawback, to me, is that the crew does all the real "fishing." They bait the hooks, set up all the rods, and set the hook when a fish hits. All we "fishermen" did was play the fish. My next ambition is to learn the tackle and lures well enough for fishing on my own, and I'd also like to buy a thirty-foot boat and just cruise the Mexican coast for a couple of seasons. Oh, and I'd also like a new Ferarri sports car, and have about as much chance of getting it.

 # TO THE SEA AGAIN: A PRIMER FOR MIDWESTERNERS

Every year, when the first snows drift over the Dakotas and into Minnesota, Iowa, Michigan, and Wisconsin, a large number of the residents of those soon-to-be-frozen countries pack up and head south, to the sunny climes of Florida, California, Mexico, and the Texas coast. There is an almost audible sigh across the south, as thousands of Midwesterners begin to thaw under the warm breezes of more tropical climes.

A few weeks later, there is again a general sigh, this time of boredom. They're more comfortable, it's true, but what is there to do? Of course, there are new places to explore, new cuisine to enjoy, and plenty of social life, but that begins to wear thin after a while, and to many of the transplants, shuffleboard and endless card games are not enough.

Many of the winter southerners are retired, and they've had to deal with lots of leisure time before. What did they do with that time? Well, many of them fished away the hours, and as they look around they discover they're in a fisherman's paradise: water, water, all around . . . but it's salty, and very different from the lakes and rivers of the Midwest. They note all the "natives" who are casting from shore, or cruising the bays in kayaks, but they don't know what they're fishing for, or what tackle or bait to use.

Some of them are too mystified to even try. Others find that the "good ol' boys" don't want to give up all their secrets, or, even if they're friendly and helpful, the fish they're describing and the rules about limits and "slots" are simply too confusing (the often-thick Southern dialect doesn't help either).

137

Those who do persevere will find that salt-water fishing is not all that difficult or different, but there are some basics that the neophyte Midwesterner has to learn.

First, this is salt water, and it means tackle must be treated a little differently. It may even mean a different reel, one that's specifically for salt water. That's not an essential, however. My old Mitchell 300 worked perfectly well for dock-and-pier fishing. It does mean that you have to be careful to clean the reel after every outing. A quick hosing-down is okay, but there are also special cleaners in spray form available at tackle stores.

While on the basic equipment, the newcomer might consider a more substantial rod and reel, as well as those specifically for salt water. I did use my standard spinning rods and reels frequently, but after a few battles with large black drums or redfish, I bought an inexpensive eight-foot surf rod and large spin-cast reel. For deep-sea fishing, even heavier equipment is required, but that is usually furnished on charter boats. More later.

Most of saltwater fishing is really pretty simple. Ninety percent of the fishing from shore or from boats in the bays abd shallow waters is bait fishing, pure and simple. There are also plenty of lures available, and there's always a "Lure of the Year" guaranteed to catch everything. Try them, but the most effective overall is probably a simple jig, which can be deadly on speckled or sea trout. For bait fishing, a double rig is often used and will work for black drum, redfish, sheepshead (which in the South is a desirable fish, unrelated to the northern rough fish.) The rig is usually fished without motion, on the bottom, or drift-fished if there's a current.

"Tails-on" shrimp for bait is available everywhere—not just bait stores, but grocery stores. Live shrimp, as well as "mud minnows" (smaller size), mullet (very large minnows), crabs, and sea lice (very like big shrimp with an attitude!) must be bought at live-bait stores, although many fishermen like taking minnows and mullet themselves with small throw-nets.

So now you have the equipment. Where do you go to fish? The answer is almost anywhere. You can surf-cast from shore, if you have bought a big two-handed rod, or from the many piers and rock jetties around any coastal bay, using whatever spinning or casting equipment you have available. Or, as you become more adventurous, you can use waders to get into somewhat deeper water or channels, or take your own small boat or kayak. There are, of course, also rental boats and charters, and that is another facet entirely.

Before you catch your first fish, read up on the game laws. You'll first want to be able to identify the fish, and then be sure it's legal. You cannot, for instance, keep any redfish except in the twenty- to thirty-inch slot—except you may keep one fifty-two-inch or more as a trophy. Similar rules apply to most species, and you'll want to carry a tape measure along any time you fish.

One of the great attractions of salt-water fishing is the amazing variety of fish available. Even fishing from shore, you may catch red or black drums, sea trout, flounder, sharks of various kinds, and a dozen others—some of them not so desirable, and you'll want to know what to do with a sting ray or hardhead catfish as well, when you hook them. (Get them off the hook without getting stung or simply cut the leader!)

You can also fish from charter boats, either bay-fishing or deep-sea, in which case you'll be fishing shoulder to shoulder with ten to twenty other fishermen, mostly Midwesterners. In both cases, tackle and bait are usually furnished. Uusually the bait will again be shrimp or mullet. If you're deep-sea fishing, of course, the variety of fish available increases dramatically: you may catch mackerel, tuna, mahi-mahi, marlin, sailfish, bonefish, and more, depending on the season and the skill of your captain.

Charter fishing is not expensive—thirty to fifty dollars a half-day most places—and you're almost guaranteed fish. On the other hand, if you want to spend a bit more, you can charter a smaller boat and guide for yourself and a few friends almost any-where on the coasts or in Mexico. This is more expensive, but it allows you to make some of the decisions about fishing—done with shrimp or minnows, usually fished on or near the bottom. The standard rig is a double or triple leader, with the sinker on the end and one or two minnows or shrimp on large hooks on the other leader(s). This is the set-up used for what you want to catch. Along the U.S. coasts this kind of charter can cost from $500 to thousands of dollars; in Mexico, a *panga* (small boat) can be chartered for $300 up. Split between three or four people, a day's fishing can still be relatively inexpensive—considering the boat crew does all the work, sets up the tackle, cleans the fish, and furnishes drinks.

With a little initiative, it's easy for the Winter Texan—or Californian, or Mexican, or Floridian—to adapt to salt-water fishing, and escape the tedium of Bingo and flea market as well as the cold weather. There's great variety, and just as at home, you can eat what you catch. You also have a number of options available once you have started, and can move from simple shore-fishing to running your own boat or taking a charter for marlin and sailfish. Give it a try, and enjoy your snow-free winters even more!

A Word About
Fishing Books

Reader: Oh, I knew this was coming!

PPR: I simply thought it appropriate to end with a few (other) good books about angling. At least I haven't given you footnotes.

Reader: I should hope not. Look, I went ahead and bought your book, and I've read a dozen others. Let's just say "The End" and go fishing.

PPR: But I feel some obligation to give you this. After all, I am a professor, and I should pass on some of my expertise for those less enlightened. However, I'll strike another bargain with you. Rather than list all the books about fishing—and there are hundreds—I will simply pick a few that are less well known. I assume everyone has read Izaak Walton, Norman MacLean, Hemingway, and those others you mentioned, so I'll skip over them and just note a few you may not have heard of. Does that strike you as fair?

Reader: Does it make any difference? You're going to do it anyway, since this is your book. Fire away, professor, and maybe I'll look at this chapter later. Right now I'm going fishing. (Exit toward the river.)

Well, should you be interested, here are a few fishing books that are not so well known, but are either instructive or just good reading.

I've always been intrigued by the fact that the very first book on fishing was written by a woman. That should not be entirely surprising, as some of the best fishers I've known, as well as the best fly-tiers, are women, but there's often the misperception that fishing is a man's game. Perhaps to the competitive types, the bass-for-prizes kind of fisherman, this is true, but for the real spirit of fishing and also some excellent advice, *The Treatise of Fishing with an Angle* is a delight. It is believed to have been written in 1496 by Dame Juliana Berners, a nun and a noblewoman, although there's some controversy about its authorship. I would like to think it's true, and I picture this medieval dame casting her well-made flies on the sparkling waters for her "dainty fish," as she describes the trout. This book is available in a beautiful edition by Lyons and Burford, with the original manuscript and a modernized version, as well as some full-color drawings of the flies described by Dame Juliana.

To complement this text, there's a collection of fly-fishing stories by women writers called *A Different Angle*. Included are some well-known writers like E. Annie Proulx and Lorian Hemingway (no relation), and almost all are passionate about fishing, although some play off the trout obsession, like Lin Sutherland's *A River Ran Over Me*. This collection is available from Berkley Books.

One of the best fishing writers of this century is the Britisher Arthur Ransome. His work is still a delight, and deals with issues including conservation that are still the concern of all serious anglers. Ransome was accomplished in so many fields that his fishing writing is sometimes overlooked. He was a literary critic, a foreign correspondent (who also married Trotsky's secretary), and the author of twelve excellent children's books, and finally a dedicated fisherman who wrote and broadcast regularly about fishing for much of his life, the articles being published in *The Manchester Guardian*. His best work, *Rod and Line*, is drawn from the *Guardian* columns, and has been called "one of the three of four most important fishing books of this century"

I don't know how many fishermen have read David James Duncan's *The River Why*, or other of his works, but even non-fishermen will appreciate his writing. *The River Why* is a coming-of-age book, a romance, and a philosophical treatise as well as a story of trout-fishing taken to the brink of insanity—and it's also hilarious. He's also very knowledgeable about fishing, so it's worth reading from every angle (sorry).

Another seldom-read book is perhaps more interesting for its authorship than for great writing. *Fishing for Fun and to Wash Your Soul* was written by Herbert Hoover, our thirty-first president, who was an advocate of the vigorous life, like Teddy Roosevelt. Hoover carried his fishing gear with him regularly, and advocated fishing for its spiritual values as well as its pleasures, as the title indicates. He does offer some interesting insights from the perspective of presidents. For instance, he says, "All presidents go fishing, even if they have never fished before, because the American people and media have respect for privacy only on two occasions. One of them is prayer, and the other is fishing, and presidents can't pray all the time." A curiosity in fishing literature, and hard to find, it's long out of print, but can be tracked down in some libraries.

Lyons and Burford publish many of the best fishing books available today, and among them is Ted Leeson's *The Habit of Rivers*. This is a collection of essays, and it explores the "interior landscape" that makes fishing, and especially fly fishing, such a powerful force. It's a wide-ranging book, but focuses finally on the Northwest coast, where Leeson lives and teaches. But that's only a part of the geography, and also only one of the subjects, all directly or indirectly linked to trout fishing but making all together a single coherent vision of fishing as a passion.

Hunting Hemingway's Trout is really not a trout-fishing book, any more than Brautigan's *Trout Fishing in America*, but the title intrigued me, it actually does have one story on the Big Two-Hearted River—but not the one that Hemingway describes, wherever that is. Lauri Anderson has set his stories in places and situations familiar to Hemingway readers, and even if it has less to do with fishing than the others here, it's a clever book and a good read.

Wayne Fields book, *What the River Knows: An Angler in Midstream* is much more focused, at least in its location. The centerpiece of the story is one stream in the Upper Peninsula (no, not the Big Two-Hearted River) and one middle-aged man's experiences and reflections on life and fishing.

Among the many books that are primarily about fishing itself, and techniques, and great experiences in the rivers of the West, Steve Raymond's *The Year of the Angler* is among the best. This is a better-known book than some of the others, and was selected by the American Booksellers Association for presentation to the White House Library. Like many classics, though, this is one that's probably talked about more than read, and it should be a must for the insights into nature and fishing, and for the clear, clean prose. It was published first in 1973 by Simon and Schuster.

And finally a very familiar name, though not often connected to fishing. In 1983 George Reiger put together a collection of fishing stories by Zane Grey, including a novel, *The Fisherman*, that had been published only in serialized form in the magazine *Outdoor America*. That long piece has a freshwater setting, while several of the other short pieces are about saltwater fishing. Grey was an enthusiastic fisherman, and although he was known for his competitiveness in almost everything else, he saw fishing as a solitary and contemplative sport, and a way to appreciate nature. It's called *The Undiscovered Zane Grey Fishing Stories*, and was published by Winchester Press under the auspices of the Izaak Walton League. Like the Hoover book, it's interesting for the insight into the character of the writer as well as for the sharp, active writing and the clear love for fishing.

PPR: I could go on and on, because fishing has held such fascination for so many writers that there are indeed a treasure-trove of such literature. Many are straight-forward how-to's: *The Compleat Lee Wulff, The Joys of Trout, Trout Fishing, Through the Fish's Eye*, and so forth, and they're valuable guides to becoming better fisherman. Others are the books of fiction and non-fiction that take fishing as their theme, or perhaps background, but are so well written that they become classics. MacLean's *A River Runs through It* is certainly one of those, and my favorite of them all, but there are others by John Gierach, Thomas McGuane, Jim Harrison and of course Hemingway. These are books that can be read with pleasure even if you're not a fisherman, but if you love the sport it gives these books an even stronger attraction.

R: And if you don't go on and on. I promise I'll read your book to this.

THE END